Open to Love

Healing Attunements and
Ceremonies for Spiritual
Adventurers

First published by O Books, 2010
O Books is an imprint of John Hunt Publishing Ltd., The Bothy, Deershot Lodge, Park Lane, Ropley,
Hants, SO24 0BE, UK
office1@o-books.net
www.o-books.net

Distribution in:

UK and Europe
Orca Book Services
orders@orcabookservices.co.uk
Tel: 01202 665432 Fax: 01202 666219
Int. code (44)

USA and Canada
NBN
custserv@nbnbooks.com
Tel: 1 800 462 6420 Fax: 1 800 338 4550

Australia and New Zealand
Brumby Books
sales@brumbybooks.com.au
Tel: 61 3 9761 5535 Fax: 61 3 9761 7095

Far East (offices in Singapore, Thailand,
Hong Kong, Taiwan)
Pansing Distribution Pte Ltd
kemal@pansing.com
Tel: 65 6319 9939 Fax: 65 6462 5761

South Africa
Stephan Phillips (pty) Ltd
Email: orders@stephanphillips.com
Tel: 27 21 4489839 Telefax: 27 21 4479879

Text copyright Jane White 2009

Design: Stuart Davies

ISBN: 978 1 84694 305 8

A CIP catalogue record for this book is available
from the British Library.

Printed by Digital Book Print

O Books operates a distinctive and ethical publishing philosophy in
all areas of its business, from its global network of authors to
production and worldwide distribution.

Open to Love

Healing Attunements and
Ceremonies for Spiritual
Adventurers

Jane White

BOOKS

Winchester, UK
Washington, USA

CONTENTS

For C

Acknowledgments

I wish to thank my family, friends and other loving helpers who have so generously given me their time and expertise, and whose support has made this book possible, in particular: my husband Paul – even though we do not speak the same spiritual language, we understand each other perfectly; Ashian Belsey, for showing me at a crucial moment in my life the way to a different reality; Linda Driver, for invaluable assistance with preparing the manuscript; Peggy Pheonix Dubro, for permission to quote from Chapter 3 of *Elegant Empowerment: Evolution of Consciousness* (Platinum Publishing); Clare Easterby, for her delightful willingness to experiment with some of the attunements, as well as her permission to share the results; Graham George, for creating such glorious artwork for the cover; Louise Hopkinson, for so many wonderful adventures and insights; John Hunt, for giving me excellent advice; Marcus Mason, for allowing me to include a brief account of his incredible experiences at Akutan; Paul McCarthy, for his guidance, calmness and trust at a rather challenging time; Ellen Mogensen, for permission to reproduce material from her website; Elaine Thompson, for permission to reproduce an extract from her book, *Voices from our Galaxy* (Bright Star Press); and Cherry Williams and Bruce Punter, for their unwavering unconditional love and gentle encouragement. A special thank you to Paul and Cherry for reading the manuscript and prompting me to get it published.

Introduction

One day my husband looked at me very intently and said, "I'd like to be able to give you some healing. Can you help me do it?" I was stunned. Paul considers himself an atheist and has never shown any inclination to explore his spirituality. Although he is one of the most compassionate and caring men I have ever had the privilege to meet, and he is undoubtedly an "old soul" who intuitively understands spiritual laws, his earthly self is adamant that, unless scientific evidence proves the contrary, an existence beyond the physical dimension we inhabit is not worth debating.

When I took my first tentative steps in spiritual healing I often used him as a guinea pig, which allowed the skeptic in him to experience energy firsthand. His rational, logical mind could not deny that the unexpected warmth flowing through my hands into his body brought relaxation and comfort.

On asking him for his view of this phenomenon, his answer came typically from the heart: "It's about loving people. If we care enough, then we should be able to help one another by transferring loving thoughts between us. We just need to know how to do it." I was not going to quibble over his beautiful explanation.

My delight at his request was diminished momentarily when he added, "But, no disrespect intended, I don't want to go on courses or do any of that reiki stuff!" This presented me with a dilemma: how could we achieve his objective without us following "rules" already laid down by experienced people in books and manuals?

Even though I had completed a range of healing courses and, despite a few raised eyebrows, had undertaken a reiki master's degree via the computer, I did not feel like a bona fide teacher. Nor did I really understand prescribed symbols and rituals sufficiently well to "attune" someone else to a recognised system. I also had to take into account Paul's desire not to be actively involved in any complicated esoteric ritual: for him it would smack too much of embarrassing metaphysical shenanigans.

Having recently been encouraged to adopt what might be described as a do-it-yourself approach to my spirituality, a solution rapidly came to mind: we could connect directly with the infinite richness of the cosmos by ourselves in our own home-made "attunement" or ceremony. I didn't give it a second thought. It seemed the most natural thing to do.

Paul agreed to leave the details to me so, relishing the chance to embark on a new venture, I sat down and wrote out a form of wording which seemed suitable for us. Excitement galloped around in my stomach: this was going to be much more ambitious than anything I had attempted before but instinctively I knew we had, as the saying goes, to fly by the seat of our pants.

Come the afternoon in question, I suggested to Paul he sit quietly, close his eyes, be willing to receive whatever might present itself and allow me to get on with what I wished to do. The room was very still and the lighting subdued as we both, in our own way, put out our requests to the universe.

I stood behind his chair and then, moving around him as the mood took me, went through "God's Gift: Opening to heal" (see Chapter 4) in my head. On reaching the end I returned to my original position and paused in anticipation.

Paul's voice broke the silence: "What next?"

Without a moment's hesitation I pointed to my back and indicated where he might place his hands. He did as asked and I staggered forward a couple of paces, nearly bumping into a wall due to the sheer force of energy which was channeled into my body.

We both stared at one another in amazement. Whatever had transpired during our little ceremony, one thing was certain: mission was accomplished, with bells on!

Life, as we know, has a habit of throwing up challenges, some pleasurable, some not so immediately welcome. When it boils down to it, they all point to a clear brief for each of us: to rediscover the light of pure or unconditional love in every fiber of our being and to integrate as much of our spiritual essence as we can.

How you do this will take you on your own very special journey which, at one time or another, will probably involve some manner of healing. That may, for instance, involve offering friendship to the lost and lonely, accepting others' differences or helping people struggling to make sense of their souls' choices.

For many, the road to abundant vitality may also include learning to honor themselves through the blessing of sickness. How often have we heard it said that disease could become a rarity if we each allowed love to fill our hearts to overflowing?

Attaining and maintaining sparkling health should be so effortless – and it can be – but if you are one of those individuals for whom it turns out to be somewhat harder than you expected (and I count myself in here), it is absolutely true that a demanding job can bring out the best in us and provide us with the greatest opportunities for growth.

Enjoying whatever fires our imagination or stimulates our senses keeps us bright-eyed and bushy-tailed too. Sometimes, though, the spark splutters and ultimately fizzles out. Dwindling hope – maybe from a lack of affection, income, options, companionship, satisfying employment or a secure spiritual bond – or having personal convictions which cause us to settle for a daily grind, can all take their toll. Reigniting our flames of passion may not seem like healing, but that in effect is what it is. It allows us to pick ourselves up out of our ruts and recapture our *joie de vivre*.

Healing, then, or harnessing the power of love to make positive change, is relevant to everyone, no matter what their background or situation. So, considering it has such huge benefits, how can we become better at it?

The answer is plain enough: through opening to the infinite Source of Love, described variously as God/Goddess/All That Is/Great Central Sun/Source/The Creator/Your greater good, etc (throughout this book use whichever you are comfortable with). In a nutshell that means accessing more and more of your own divine self. Facets of you exist on numerous levels within "dimensions" or continuum of consciousness. By re-establishing a mindful link with them, integrating some of their energetic resonances, and then bringing everything into balance, you can draw upon enormous depths of compassion and creativity you may not yet realize you have at your fingertips.

This is what may be called "multi-dimensional" healing, for restoration to wholeness does not take place only on the earth plane: repercussions of what you do in this dimension impact on your presence in each of the other dimensions. Such healing involves exploring the intelligence of eternal Love, the divine Light within you which connects you with your children, partner, friends, animals, angels, crystals, faeries, Gaia, ascended masters, cosmic energies, the elohim and so on – in other words with the entirety of creation.

Multi-dimensional healing also encourages you to expand your mind and heart until you *really* comprehend why, as divine beings, we are each cherished, we are all as one, and we are worthy of the finest this and further worlds have to offer.

My interest in such healing grew from letting go of chronic illness. Rather than depending on others to sort out my problems for me, I was directed to stand on my own two feet and to take back the power I was for ever giving away. Bolstered by the success of Paul's attunement and following my intuition, I devised a series of simple ceremonies which, despite their lack of obvious complexity, proved utterly transformational. I entered realms I had never dreamed of and within a comparatively short period began at long last to appreciate the gift of experiencing Spirit through a human body.

The time has now come to share some of those attunements, together with the concepts behind them so that you can make your own informed choices. I'm also including a scattering of personal anecdotes to help put them into context.

Blessed by the ascended realms of Love and Light to carry high vibrational energy for anyone who chooses to work with them, these attunements are intended for initiating new phases of learning and healing according to your truth and reality. You can take them as they are, once or several times, or you can adapt them as you see fit. They can be used to great effect by groups too. (As humanity continues to evolve, the coming together of enlightened people with a common purpose that is underpinned by unconditional love will accomplish far greater achievements than has been possible in the past.)

It does not matter how precisely or vaguely you incorporate the ceremonies into your life. I feel it is my job merely to point out possibilities, to suggest different, perhaps unconventional, ways of developing yourself which will appeal to the adventurer in you.

They are designed to be fun tools which enable you to develop an intimate relationship with your higher wisdom. It is my hope that they inspire you to go on and create your own, thereby demonstrating for yourself how immeasurably powerful, precious and remarkable a being of Love you are.

Blessings always.

Chapter 1

Creating attunements

Honoring the divine in yourself

Creating the best for yourself is really a case of ignoring every-thing you have learned, been told or gone through which places a restriction on you.

An obvious example of self-limitation is when people resort to saying "I can't do such and such," or "That type of thing doesn't happen to me..." "I can't," in the sense of "can't achieve it because it's too hard" or "I'm not good enough," would be better off out of our vocabulary altogether. You can do anything your imagination conjures – and more – as long as it is fueled by love, sincerity and joy and, if necessary, you are prepared to put in a little effort.

Self-attunements and ceremonies are a way of making known through positive action your heart's desires, and then manifesting them, sometimes extremely quickly, with the universe's help. They focus and magnify your intent, rather like you putting up a gigantic poster to advertise an event you are organizing. Your unique request or message, vibrant with your enthusiasm and vision, is unmissable. Those who are interested in what you are doing know you mean business and will be drawn like a magnet to you in full support of you and your enter-prise.

If you tend to put others first or believe that someone else will have the answers because they have been around the block a few more times than you have, then a special ritual arranged by you for you is also a means to prove to yourself how deserving and capable a being you are.

Each time you perform a ceremony you establish a link and

7

communicate directly with the spiritual realms, most notably with your divine "higher" self from whom you may receive a direct response (hence the phrase "self-attunement" – literally tuning in to your divinity). This may, for example, be through inspiring thoughts and feelings or the imparting of information in order to prepare you for your next steps.

Over time your link will become stronger and clearer until you attain a regular, conscious connection with what you will soon realize are other parts of yourself in other dimensions. You will then understand that the reason you are being propelled along at speed, being showered with largesse along the way, is mainly due to your own volition. And with that you will also discover that the best person in the world to ask for advice is you.

This is not to say there won't be occasions when you would rather go to a workshop, experience attunements carried out by someone else, read an inspirational book, see a therapist or pick the brains of like-minded friends. Life would be very tedious if we did not interact with other people on the planet and share our pleasures and laughter, sorrows and doubts as well as our talents. We are all teachers and pupils, givers and receivers, and sometimes there is a choice to be made between doing it yourself and going elsewhere for assistance (more about this later).

However, once you have gleaned as much as you can from external sources and you are still not making the progress you would like, it may be a sign to retire on your own for a while. If this sounds alarming and the old refrain of "No, can't possibly do it!" pipes up, you may have prompted your resisting self to dig its heels in again. As *Star Trek* fans know, "Resistance is futile!" With a degree of encouragement, the scaredy-cat who is frightened of moving on can usually be coaxed out into the sunshine for a welcome change of scene.

There is no escaping the fact that there are some things in life which only we can accomplish for ourselves, but the cracking of tough nuts brings an incredible sense of achievement. Although it can seem as though we are completely on our own, there are unseen forces at work applauding us, bringing special events and people into our lives, and helping us become all that we can be.

Technically we are never alone, and we have only to take the initiative and ask for help for it to be provided. Our ceremonies, unique to each of us, demonstrate to the spiritual realms just how genuine our requests are.

Setting the scene

With a modicum of thought and preparation beforehand, you can make each and every ceremony a memorable occasion. Some people like the thrill of being outdoors, while others prefer to be inside. Whatever your usual spiritual practices, spend a few minutes thinking laterally to see if an alternative is more suitable.

For example, if you are most accustomed to meditating in the comfort of your own home and you would like to attune with the faerie kingdom, a spot of research to find a pretty place in nature nearby for your ceremony is going to be highly regarded by the beings you are intending to contact.

Anyone who has traveled to a foreign country will know how pleased locals can be when you are appreciative of their culture or try speaking a few words in their language – even if you make a hash of it, your attempts are warmly received and people are more disposed to put themselves out for you. The same is true in spiritual circles: that extra you put into considering others will be reciprocated. Trust can be strengthened on both sides of the celestial bridge.

If you're new to such matters and don't have any particular routines, making an altar or point of focus might be a good starting point. It can be as straightforward as covering a small table with a brightly-colored cloth, and arranging a few items on top. Depending on the theme of the ceremony, you might choose symbolic objects, however weird or exotic, to put on your table.

I might include a couple of fossils from my collection to denote the eternal energies of Creation; a teddy bear to represent the animal kingdom; a much loved, large plastic kingfisher, bought for me by my stepfather, in recognition of messengers from Spirit; a piece of moldavite to remind me of galactic and cosmic friends...

Whatever takes my mood to honor the beings with whom I am collaborating will be taken out of a cupboard or off a shelf. I sometimes wonder what a visitor would say if they walked in and saw me sitting on the floor in front of a huge chunk of rock and a host of cuddly toys!

And talking of furry creatures, how many times have I shut the door before a ceremony only to hear scratching and miaowing outside within seconds. These days I leave the door slightly ajar so that a nosy cat on the prowl does not feel left out (humans are given strict instructions to keep away). In fact there have been occasions when I have wondered whether a cat might have been making its own contribution to the proceedings by sitting quietly in an unusual place or touching my body at precise points, often chakra positions.

Animals are working with and on behalf of humanity to bring in and ground certain energies, so we should not be surprised by such behavior. Friends of mine were once "gonged" by a healer whose dog always lay in the same room as the healer's clients and slept peacefully throughout the incredibly noisy sessions. It took them many months to deal with the issues which surfaced as a result of their gonging, so I can only assume the dog was as clear as a proverbial bell and an assistant of sorts for his human companion.

You can treat this special time as an opportunity to enjoy yourself and feast your senses – learning to heighten each of them is a way into developing spiritual gifts. Music can bring a soothing atmosphere to the proceedings and allow you to be "in the moment", banishing from your mind thoughts of the evening meal or the forthcoming parents' night at school. A few scented flowers never go amiss, while a candle to symbolize the Light of God within you always sets off a room nicely.

But really all that matters is that you create a space which is meaningful to you. Whether you prefer a hundred accessories or none is unimportant. The key is whether your heart is in the right place.

Preparing yourself

Ideally a spiritual ceremony is best conducted when you have planned for it and you are feeling relaxed, calm, not too tired and have at least an hour to spare. Sometimes, though, it is not possible to meet all of these criteria. Heavy work loads, family commitments, poor health or even a spontaneous burst of inspiration can wreak havoc with the best of intentions and you may have to seize an opportune moment when it arises.

Even in these circumstances you can still whip out a candle and put on some music before spending an extra few minutes concentrating on your breathing and generally calming your mind, body and emotions.

Using a violet flame invocation at this point will give you a quick spiritual rub down too and help clear communication channels, which is excellent preparation for what is to come. The violet flame, associated with the seventh divine ray, is a universal transmutational force which has the power to cleanse and convert through its alchemy lower vibrational energy to a higher form. It has a cumulative effect, so the more you invoke it the greater its impact will be.

Some people also opt for a protection invocation before embarking on any spiritual connection and, come to that, for general interactions throughout the day. I went through a period in which I did not bother with protection, as it seemed to me that if I were confident in myself and the strength of my Light, then that was sufficient. But a strange incident convinced me that perhaps I needed to reassess my assumptions.

A close relative used to visit regularly and I would invariably find myself feeling the need to cross my arms and legs in a very defensive manner. For years I wrestled with my reaction: we did not have the easiest of relationships and we did not always see eye to eye, but I knew this person to be a great teacher for me and we loved each other dearly.

One afternoon, as we sat and talked, I became aware psychically of a tube, like a garden hose, hooked into my heart chakra. I was so taken aback that I blinked quickly and the image was gone. Irrespective of where the other end of the tube was (I did not wish to apportion blame to my relative), the mere fact that I had become aware of it was sufficient to make me reconsider the question of protection and also what lessons I was being presented with.

The very next morning a friend rang and for some reason the conversation soon turned to protection. After I relayed the story of the hose, Cherry, a Light channeler of Sanat Kumara, agreed that the invocations we had both been using were perhaps, if we were honest with ourselves, somewhat fear-based. We therefore came up with an alternative which is centered around love of all beings, however much or little Light they are carrying. Here is a version for anyone thinking about a new protection decree (if you're not keen on the phrase "protect me" and its associations, you could substitute "restore me to wholeness" instead):

May the radiance of Divine Love enfold and embrace me now (*and/or* throughout today and tonight), to heal and protect me, and to sustain the purity of my sacred space. May those I encounter receive, through divine Light and Grace, an abundance of blessings for themselves and may they in turn convey blessings to those they meet. Thank you. So be it.

Composing attunements

After taking some of the attunements in this book and getting the hang of them, you might wish to try your hand at your own. The desire for a ceremony may emerge gradually during ongoing spiritual practice or it may arrive suddenly out of thin air – a case of being uplifted one minute and needing to organize something the next.

Your aim is to be as clear as possible within yourself about what exactly it is you wish to achieve or ask for. Clarity is a great virtue and one we can cultivate easily by combining logical thinking, current spiritual knowledge and intuition.

Such dedicated focus will make for a much brighter advertising poster than muddled messages. If you are not sure what it is that you are requesting, the universe may give you a surprising response as it tries to make sense of your publicity campaign. You can always include a caveat to cover yourself for circumstances you may not yet have considered.

You may be the sort of person who prefers to jot down ideas several days beforehand so that you have time to mull over them and can tweak here and there. Or you may prefer to go on impulse on the day. Express what you feel in whatever way is meaningful for you, and you won't go far wrong. You don't have to be the world's best author, poet or songwriter. If you can develop the knack of stilling your mind, connecting with your heart center (in the middle of your chest) and listening to the impulses emanating from your higher wisdom, this can be hugely beneficial.

There is something to be said for writing down whatever comes into your head, without censoring it. This allows you to free up your thinking – to enable your lower and higher minds to work together in harmony. You can then edit afterwards if need be.

And remember: there are no limits to what you can ask for in humility and with the purest of motives. Quite often we are restricted because we simply do not know whether something is possible or that it even exists. Anything is possible. Brainstorm outside your usual zones and reach for the stars – and beyond.

Having had a Christian upbringing, I am reminded at this juncture of a memorable phrase from the Bible "...and the Word was God" (John chapter 1, verse 1). In a carefree moment it set me reflecting on how, as individuated sparks from Mother/Father God and co-creators, the words we use – the energy generated by each of us – are divine, and as such are very powerful. They have the capacity within a split second to promote goodness or increase darkness.

This is why it is incumbent on us to choose carefully wherever possible our thoughts, speech and even what messages we send to one another. Once we have achieved mastery of those skills then perhaps telepathy, which works best on loving frequencies, can once more come to the fore.

Continuing this theme, I can vouch for the enormous long-term effect of words uttered with passion and conviction. One afternoon, using a technique I shall describe in the next chapter, I was concentrating hard on a health goal whose manifestation I believed was being blocked. After a couple of minutes a distinct, rather strange phrase entered my head. Then my eyes brimmed with tears as concealed emotions suddenly surfaced.

I had never come across this expression before, but the feelings were real enough so I knew there must be truth behind it. I switched on the computer, went onto the internet and searched for a relevant site. Within seconds there printed on the screen in front of me as confirmation was the very same phrase I had heard in my mind: "vow of suffering". I knew of such vows as chastity and silence taken by devotees in religious institutions, but not one of suffering.

I scanned the text, eagerly taking in the information: "Vows of suffering and retribution are among the most toxic that are carried over from past lives. The myth underlying is that the body and mind are impediments to spiritual progress and must be 'chastened, mortified, and delivered into submission'."

Reading on, I noted the suggestion that each vow has a connection with a particular chakra, in this case the third eye, and that the vow of suffering "can paralyze one into an inactive, joyless existence", in some cases to self-mutilation.

If, before embarking full-time on a spiritual tack, I had had to give an overview of my life, which had ground to a halt through debilitating, painful illness and emotional and mental fatigue, it could easily have been described by the end of that very sentence: "inactive joyless existence" or, to be more precise, "suffering".

I eased myself back in my chair to absorb the curious facts. This surely was indeed a remnant from a past life that was surfacing. How extraordinary that it should still be impacting on my current life.

Shortly afterwards I decided, via input from higher guidance, that the best course of action to deal with this situation was to say out loud (the out loud part seemed most important) three times: "I hereby renounce my vow of suffering."

You would not believe how difficult it was for me to open my mouth. It felt like an absolutely massive act of betrayal. I had to come to terms with the fact that a sacred commitment to behave in a certain way indefinitely (from my perspective at the time the commitment was made) was now being cancelled. I grieved for the me that had made such an impactful decision in the first place, and which now felt foolish as well as reluctant to let go.

If any of these experiences set bells ringing with you, it might be worth investigating this possible aspect of your own previous life or lives. Anyone who has taken an oath in the past as a shaman, to share the pain and suffering of animals, may feel ready to release themselves from that responsibility too. I will return briefly to the subject in later chapters, but for the moment I would advocate the following, spoken aloud three times with conviction, to start the healing process. Speaking out parallels the original ceremony, when you would probably have voiced statements in front of others; your witness now is your divine self:

> Through Divine Grace and All That I Am, and in the Name of Love, I hereby renounce every vow and oath (*or, ideally, use specific names if you know them*) I have taken in any lifetime in any time frame and in any dimension and alternative reality that no longer serves my highest good. I invoke the Violet Flame to transmute the words, feelings and sacred energy of my original statements of intent into Light. May restorative healing now flow freely through my being.
>
> With the Creator's blessing, may I be shown joyful new ways of helping other beings which honor and respect our magnificence, power and godliness, and which are to the benefit and delight of all. Thank you.
>
> So be it. So it is done. So it is.

Now, back to a few notes you may like to consider when you organize material for your own attunements and ceremonies. They are just guidelines – you may decide not to write anything down at all and trust that suitable words will flow from your mouth when the time comes. This approach can be good for communicating depth of feeling. On the other hand the advantage of having a piece of paper in front of you is that it enables you to remember what you wish to say, and you can speak or sing with power and authority.

If you go through your text three times, you ensure a solid build-up of energy – and three, of course, is also a sacred number. Were you to change your mind and alter the wording of your request each time, the universe might be confused by potentially conflicting messages and its response as a consequence might be muted.

We all know that intent plays an enormous part in spirituality but, as I have already mentioned, precision in how we express ourselves and communicate generally is also becoming increasingly important. As Masters of Light we are expected to take much greater personal responsibility than perhaps we may have been accustomed to in the past. In this respect anyone putting themselves forward for a bump up the so-called spiritual ladder, which is what self-attunements are all about, should note that speedy advancement will often involve corresponding healing work in their inner and outer worlds. If you are to sustain your new, higher vibration, you will inevitably have to discard or transform your old, lower vibrational energies which no longer match it or are no longer appropriate for you.

Try therefore to be as balanced as possible before each attunement, and certainly if you are attempting a succession of leaps in one go. That way the ride will be relatively smooth as denser energies of your being surface to be transformed at an agreeable pace. (Chapter 4 has more information on this topic.)

Wording

Here is a list of headings for the type of content you might include. It is a rather formulaic approach, but it may help give some structure for your ideas. As always, take what you like, leave the rest and plug the gaps with your own inventions. Eventually you may wish to do something completely different in keeping with your personal vision.

If you are leading a group, you could make the attunement part of a guided meditation, perhaps taking people in their imagination to a place of immense beauty, such as a magical forest or a crystal temple, where highly evolved spiritual beings welcome them and assist them with their development. And, if you're comfortable doing so, you could ask the spiritual realms beforehand how they might wish to be involved – they may bring gifts for the occasion. You can also prepare a special meditation for yourself.

Express gratitude

Starting with an acknowledgment of our Creator and the blessings received each day shows a genuine appreciation of life's wealth and abundance. When the going is tough it is easy to forget that from a higher perspective everything that comes our way is a gift of one sort or another. The more we enjoy ourselves, the more we will attract to ourselves treasures to keep our souls singing.

Connect with your divine self

If you place yourself in the hands of your "higher self", your discarnate all-knowing self, you can be assured that everything which transpires will be the best for you. It knows how far to push you, and when to ease back on the throttle.

Invite other helpers from the spiritual realms

Politeness never goes amiss. If you are unfamiliar with the spiritual "hierarchy" or you are not sure who is currently working with you (not all beings/energies have names), you may simply wish to call upon, as an example, some of the following to assist you: your guardian angel, angels and archangels (of healing, abundance, compassion, peace, etc), ascended masters, cosmic beings of Love and Light, faeries, crystal masters, gatekeepers, animal devas, Mother Earth.

You may at times prefer solely to connect directly with Source/God/All That Is/Mother/Father God (or whichever phrase you prefer to use), without any intervention from other spiritual mentors, guides, companions and co-workers.

Invoke the violet flame

Even if you have already done this as part of your preparation, another swirl will dispel any lingering lower vibrational doubts. "I AM the Violet Flame and Fire of Light" is a useful affirmation to employ here, the addition of "Fire" being especially efficacious as it has an even greater potency than the flame.

Make your attunement request/outline your desire or intention

If you preface your request with such phrases as "Through All That I Am, through Divine Light and Grace and in the Name of God and Love..." you cover yourself against inadvertently instigating something which might accrue negative karma or which is not in your highest interests. You are asking to receive within the blessing of divine laws.

Your "desire or intention" might be to send love to everyone you know, to celebrate the joys of life, to show gratitude in a particular way for your blessings... You are not necessarily asking for anything here, merely using a ceremony to convey your sentiments.

Thank your helpers

Know that much will be being organized on your behalf and, although you may not comprehend the nature of the activity, a quiet "thank you" would be in order.

Surrender to Love

At the end of the ceremony you could offer a few more words of gratitude and concentrate on generating a feeling of trust within your physical self. Surrender involves you lovingly handing over your requests with grace and in faith. You might also try to imagine how you will be when your wish is fulfilled. Once you have felt in your heart that which you are hoping to achieve, it is easier to co-create it: it becomes a reality rather than a possibility.

Seal and bless the occasion

You can wrap up with "Let it be so," "Amen," or your favored equivalent.

After the attunement/ceremony

I recommend that you spend about half an hour after the attunement resting or meditating. Sometimes you will be aware of information being transmitted to you, or your body may respond to energies as you are being worked on. It is worth having a notepad within reach for recording your experiences: images, feelings and sensations may not mean much at the time, but can provide eureka moments later on.

Manipulation of your energetic make-up may continue throughout the rest of the day and during the night when you are most relaxed and receptive. Again, record anything out of the ordinary, as it may offer valuable insights.

Results may be instant or they may take hours, days, weeks or even, in some cases, months. They may happen as you had hoped for, or they may materialize in a most unexpected manner. Alternatively, you may be presented with circumstances that apparently bear no relevance to your ceremony. Be patient. You have been heard. This scenario usually comes about because there are further stages for you to go through before you can manifest your dream, and you may in fact discover that they lead you to a better outcome than the one you had planned.

If there is inner cleansing to be done, try not to get bogged down by frustration. It is merely a transitory but essential clearing phase – like switching on the defogger in the car on a winter morning. Once the condensation has evaporated, the glass is again transparent and you can see where you are going.

Allow yourself plenty of integration time. Subtle bodies can become temporarily out of alignment (use the affirmations in Chapter 3 to help rebalance them) and your physical body may feel tired or over-stimulated. Suitable pampering won't go amiss, so give yourself a few treats.

In addition, remain open to continued learning. Just because you have reached a different vantage point on your path does not necessarily mean you yet know how you got there. Integration is also about absorbing information from books, friends and so on, which deepens your understanding of the trail you are blazing into new areas. Once you have achieved comprehension on every level, then you are ready for your next attunement.

Note

The attunements in this book can be taken more than once over an extended period. This allows you to integrate a large amount of data in incremental stages. My advice regarding timing is to go with whatever feels right for you, also bearing in mind how much work on yourself you are prepared to put in should that prove necessary. Finally, it might seem an obvious comment to make, but if you treat an attunement as a bit of a joke and merely go through the motions, perhaps because you think it's something you ought to do rather than you wish to do or you want to please someone else, the universe may not necessarily play ball. But if your desire is sincere and heartfelt, no matter how simply you express yourself, it will pull all the stops out for you.

Chapter 2

In your own words...

Before going much further I should like to offer you a sacred gift, an ancient healing technique for accessing and clearing out lower vibrational clutter you may not even be aware you have. It can be used to seek out the root causes of illness, phobias, lack of abundance, behavior or thought patterns you would rather not have, and other ongoing challenges – tiny or large – in your life. It can also help to redress imbalances at higher spiritual levels or reveal why you feel particularly passionately about certain apparent inequities in the world.

Because of this it can play a significant part in any stage of spiritual development, and complements attunements very well – although in a sense it can be considered a "self-attunement" in its own right, since it helps you listen and act upon your own inner messages and truths.

It was passed on from spiritual masters to Ashian Belsey, an inspirational lady who at one time received personal one-on-one teaching, including this technique, from various ascended beings who appeared to her in person (unfortunately, Ashian's book *Beyond Fear* in which she talks about her remarkable experiences is no longer in print). Ashian then shared her knowledge with some local healing groups, which is how I met her. My heartfelt thanks to her for allowing me, in turn, to share my version and insights with you.

As a slight digression, it is probably fair to say that of the transformational tools currently circulating the globe, similar ones can appear in seemingly different guises. Old souls, now remembering what was once common wisdom, are bringing to our attention much past knowledge that is of relevance for the twenty-first century. It is no coincidence that this is happening at a time when humanity is taking such huge strides forwards in its evolution. However, if you stripped these tools down to the basics, you would probably find that many were minor variations on a single universal theme whose focus is to assist us to pare away fear and replace it with love.

The proliferation of these aids is partly due to the fact that everyone has their own spin on how something should be done, and what suits one person may not necessarily suit another – human beings need a wide range of approaches to match their diverse cultures. We have to take account of people's ingenuity too: original methods can be greatly modified through experimentation.

This sort of marvelous co-creation always reminds me of cooking. Lots of people do not follow recipes precisely, preferring instead to adapt according to their household's tastes and to the ingredients they happen to have in their cupboards and fridges. While maintaining respect for the chefs who created the recipes, they still like to push the boat out a little and go wherever imagination takes them to produce mouth-watering dishes which may become family favourites that are passed down to future generations.

The same holds for spiritual techniques. It can be thrilling to find out how far you can push supposed boundaries. This approach does not devalue a tool and neither is it disrespectful to the being who introduced you to it. There is never a right or a wrong way of doing anything, just the one we discern suits each of us best in a particular moment. We may call upon any number of aids in any number of combinations throughout our lives.

I mention this by way of an introductory explanation, since the information I am about to present to you comes from my interpretation and lengthy exploration over many years of what I now call "Word Power", a phrase I coined to avoid repeating "that ascended master technique Ashian told me about"!

The underlying principles are based on spiritual laws and therefore are, as you would expect, very simple. Their effects nonetheless can be profound, so it is worth taking a moment or two to grasp the essentials. Once you have done that, you can then decide whether to pursue Word Power for yourself and, if so, how to mould it to fit your own operating style – and to pass it on to others!

Word Power

Word Power, or whatever name you choose to give this form of healing, is a means of getting in touch with deeper levels of your consciousness via your body. Not only does your physical body constantly receive messages from your subtle bodies and your higher wisdom, it also carries denser energy, codes and imprints in its cells and DNA of unresolved emotions and such like from your current and past lives which it knows are creating discord for you. These may manifest as various forms of dis-ease.

Our bodies are like books written in an old language we may have forgotten how to read. Word Power provides the means of deciphering it and therefore of discovering our true healing needs. Once you have got the knack of it, it is very easy – although it does require honesty, a certain amount of commitment depending on how far you wish to take it, and a real desire to conquer your bugbears great or small. Even if you have been on your spiritual path for a while, there is usually something you can profitably review. Life is a never-ending round of shedding ever finer layers of ourselves.

Through using Word Power and invoking the violet flame you create a safe, sacred space in which you can be yourself without fear of karmic payback. Some people worry that if they use indecently colorful language during a session, then they will accrue bad karma. This is not the case: if you find yourself shrieking obscenities at the top of your voice, you will undoubtedly be releasing anger as an important part of your healing. Such behavior is nothing to be embarrassed about: acknowledging a previously concealed well of misery or resentment can be very beneficial. And in any case the violet flame will soon mop up after you.

Incidentally, swearing is apparently related to the side of the brain which handles emotions. Other verbal communication is connected to the non-emotional side. This is why many normally polite people may have an uncharacteristic outburst when suddenly confronted by an unexpected turn of events. It is a perfectly natural reaction to possible stress.

Problems may arise when individuals become addicted to the chemical rush in their bodies that is created when powerful, sometimes potentially destructive, emotions are allowed to take the driving seat for much of the time. On the flip side of the coin, suppressing feelings and never giving them an appropriate outlet is not the healthiest of solutions either, as this can store up trouble for the future. The answer, I suppose, is wherever possible to infuse what we say with heart-felt love. That way, both sides of our brains will be functioning together in a balanced, positive manner.

If you practice Word Power regularly it will become second nature as you learn to attune instantly to your body and recognize when it has messages for you. They may not necessarily be about physical health but may be pointers to an area in your life, such as relationships, work, hobbies and your personal growth, where high vibrational energy is not flowing as freely as it might. When a message arrives, perhaps through an unusual, unfamiliar sensation or a noticeable reaction to a casually spoken word or phrase, you do not need to be anywhere special to decode it, but privacy is usually preferable.

While you are becoming accustomed to the process, I recommend something along the following lines for the first few sessions. Read through to the end of these notes to familiarize yourself with the technique beforehand and, if you feel it would be helpful to have a friend with you, ask them to read this section too so that they have an understanding of what you are about to undertake.

Please note that if you are emotionally or mentally fragile or unwell at the moment, it would be best to wait until you are fit again, or at least until you have plenty of support (of the human variety!), before trying out Word Power. This comment isn't meant to frighten you, it's just that the process may stir up feelings you may not wish or be fully equipped to handle right now.

On the general question of health, it goes without saying that should you have concerns about any aspect of your wellbeing, or you have a complaint that is not improving, contact your local professional healthcare providers for their advice. You can then decide what is the right course of action for you to take, whether that be complementary therapy or conventional medical treatment, or a combination of the two.

Once you have tried Word Power several times, and have perhaps experimented with a few of the suggestions outlined later, play around with it and, if you want to, find out how you can develop it further. I am sure it will continue in some shape or form to have a valuable role during the new Aquarian age.

Making it happen

Choose a calm, favourite spot where you will be undisturbed for around half an hour or so – preferably pick a time of day when you are most alert and not physically taxed.

At first you may find that background music, even calming, meditation-type music, is more of a distraction than an aid to concentration. But it is very much personal preference. What I would say is that, as you need to focus one hundred per cent attention on yourself in what might be called a "working meditation", a quiet environment can sometimes prevent you from becoming side-tracked.

Prepare yourself and your surroundings by decreeing three times:

"Through All that I Am, I invoke the Violet Flame to transmute the energies in and around me and to transform them into Light,"

or, if it feels right for you,

"I AM the Violet Flame."

You might also imagine a violet cloud whirling round you and moving into every corner of the room – as mentioned earlier, being the spiritual equivalent of a third-dimensional cleansing fire, the violet flame purifies, heals and clears everything it encounters. You can ask for it to be present throughout your session if you wish, which will give you additional help and encouragement.

Lie or sit comfortably, with your eyes shut: it is important to keep your eyes closed, because opening them can cause you to disconnect from your higher guidance. If you wear glasses, remove them beforehand to give you complete freedom of movement.

Ask your divine self and guides in the spiritual dimensions for their assistance and inspiration. Remember that you can stop at any moment – you are always in control – but try to keep going until you have reached a natural conclusion.

An aspect of you that fears change and is happy with the current status quo may attempt to disorientate you and persuade you that you are too tired. Or you may suddenly feel you cannot be bothered. These are positive signs, because they mean there are important matters to attend to. Gently, but firmly, tell yourself that you have set aside this precious time and you are not going until you have made progress. Also have the aim of making it easy and enjoyable for yourself.

Bring to the fore what it is that you wish to inquire into, for instance, why you have been presented with your current set of challenges, why your health or work are not particularly rosy, why you always respond in a certain way to other people's comments about you... Then set your intent to get to the bottom of the conundrum and to heal yourself, asking for your highest good and to be connected to your higher wisdom.

You can begin by reminding yourself how you are, such as:

"I'm cross with my neighbor, but I don't know why,"
"I'm sad,"
"I still feel jealous of my ex,"
"I fear what will happen to me in later years," or
"I've lost touch with my spirituality."

Or you can look at specific ailments:

"I have a sore knee."
"I have mouth ulcers."
"I have migraines regularly."

Much emphasis in spiritual circles is placed upon always remaining upbeat, so it may seem to go against the grain to verbalize so-called negative statements about yourself. However, spirituality is about taking control of your life through being truthful, and the only way you can really do that is to allow Light to shine into every nook and cranny. Hiding skeletons in cupboards will only hold you back, and sometimes the best policy is to yank those cupboard doors open and brazenly face the contents. They can then be cleaned out in a flash.

The beauty of Word Power is that even if you do not consider yourself a touchy-feely sort of person or you are not yet familiar with the inner you, you can still set the ball rolling by analyzing your situation and making very brief, matter-of-fact statements about it. For example, you could start with:

"I'm not vastly wealthy,"
"I don't have loads of friends," or
"I'm not manifesting the best for myself."

You may not be overly concerned about your current state of affairs, but nevertheless these sentences represent aspects you would like to improve. Having the purest of motives – to create a better "now" for yourself – is everything here. These seemingly nondescript phrases, which you can soon shorten or rearrange to concentrate on specific words, will act as catalysts. They kick-start a chain of events which will lead you deep into your consciousness or "inner knowing" which holds information and memories of what, through the manifestation of your challenges, environment and the workings of your body, is being brought to your attention for healing.

Repeat your phrase, again and again without pausing (except for breath!), preferably out loud or, if you can maintain your focus, in your head. Concentrate on the words and, if you are finding there are too many of them, pick out those which seem to be the most meaningful for you. You might start with:

"I fear going to my friend's house because of what they might say to me"

and condense first to:

"I fear going to my friend's,"

and then:

"Fear friend, fear friend, fear friend..."

29

At the same time tune in to your body for physical sensations, emotions and feelings, however slight. You might notice unfamiliar areas of discomfort or an odd uneasiness. Stay with them as far as you can. These are confirmatory signposts telling you that you are moving in the right direction.

If a new phrase pops into your mind use that, however strange it seems. Trust it, and repeat it over and over. Repetition maintains focus and prevents any unwanted thoughts, such as what groceries you need, from sneaking in. In a way it is also a form of sound or vibrational therapy – the frequencies will begin to work on your make-up, loosening your hold of denser energetic material, which is why your unusual sensations may begin to show themselves.

Always be *honest* with yourself and, if they arise, admit your fears and guilt or what you do not currently like about yourself. You are probably aware that these are blessed gifts from which you can often learn the most about yourself, but sometimes we are very good at ignoring them or pretending to ourselves that they don't exist because we don't like how they appear or how they make us behave. Anything you would rather avoid is what needs to be faced for the benefit of your progress.

Keep scanning yourself and playing around with your phrases. Whatever your range of physical and emotional responses, be open to the unique experiences which are presenting themselves to you and make them even more pronounced. The best way of doing that is to use only those words which resonate with you at a deep level to describe as accurately as possible the sensations, ultimately the emotions, you are feeling in each second. For instance, if you start with:

"I have a sore knee," or
"I'm envious of other people's gifts," or
"I can't tune in to my clairvoyance," or
"Will doesn't like me,"

but become aware of acute frustration welling up inside you, move on to:

"I'm frustrated,"

and then home in on the source of your frustration, perhaps:

"I'm frustrated with myself for being stingy."

Try not to dissect the situation into masses of minute, intricate details: only describe what you are feeling – and feel it as fully as you can.

Keep the phrases flowing. They are rather like an interface between your body and your higher self. You may find that changing individual words and even repeating segments of words can help sustain, often quicken, the momentum, for example:

"He was un... un... un... help... help... help... ful... ful... ful to me."

Eventually one magic word or phrase, such as:

"I feel guilty for what I did"

will hit you with some force and this will be the final key to cracking the code. You will immediately access the current dominant underlying cause of your problem issue and you may also be acutely aware of a vibrant, close connection with your divine self, which in itself can stimulate great healing.

You will know when you have struck the jackpot because you will in all likelihood face strong emotion, sometimes in an extremely forceful way. This can be anything from sorrow, fear and anger to immense happiness and love. Whatever it is, embrace it fully, feel it and breathe deeply. You may also experience a physical release of energy.

Next steps

As you maintain your link with your higher wisdom, you will know precisely what steps to take next in order to bring about permanent healing and a lasting change in yourself (if for any reason you are unsure or out of your depth, ask for direction from your helpers).

This may initially involve crying, shouting, hitting a cushion, acknowledging your worthiness, whooping with joy... Say, shout or do whatever you want to in the moment, trusting your inner guidance. However unpleasant the process may be, remain determined to resolve inner turmoil by feeling the emotion to the full. You will then be ready for the following stage of Word Power when restorative laughter, unconditional love, forgiveness, compassion and love of Mother/Father God will be brought to the fore for you.

At that point you will be able to create a form of words – a positive affirmation if you like – which you can repeat over and over in the same way as before, although now you will be reprogramming yourself with a new way of being rather than trying to access and remove an old program. After that you will ultimately reach a place of stillness and peace which you can revisit at any time in the future.

It is interesting to note here that, even though you may have believed for a long time that you love yourself, are worthy of abundance, etc, Word Power can reveal layers of yourself which are not actually in total alignment with your thinking. By greeting them, you deepen and strengthen your unconditional love for yourself.

If you are a visual sort of person, you can use your imagination to rewrite the past or to resolve difficulties at the very point at which they occurred – as long as you keep feeling through the process rather than getting stuck in the whys and wherefores of old dramas. Make new, rosy scenarios that cater for your and, if necessary, other beings' needs – always aim for a "win-win" situation. To lighten proceedings a little you might make yourself and other people cartoon characters who perform incredible feats. Humor puts the bleakest of predicaments into perspective: everything you have ever done or had done to you has been chosen by your soul as an opportunity for advancement and expansion.

Supposing you were stabbed in a previous life, you could visualize removing the dagger from your body and transforming it into a plastic knife. Looking your attacker in the face, you might then burst into laughter at the huge joke. By this stage the blood on your skin might be tomato sauce, and your attacker might also be having a fit of the giggles. You then embrace in friendship, the animosity between you dissolved for ever.

At all times you have the power, ability and creativity to do absolutely anything. For instance, if you find yourself mentally reliving a situation in which you were unable to stand up for yourself, this time take the initiative and speak up. Explain that you are not going to die a horrible death because of someone else's desire for revenge/put up with insults/be forced to do something against your will, etc. You are going to take the lead and restore harmony and goodwill. Aggressors usually back down immediately and are keen to reconcile themselves with you in love. And if you can imagine being in their shoes, it makes it easier for you to understand and forgive them.

Move with the flow. Should memories surface about a past incident you regret but which you would now like to rectify, say "I forgive myself" meaningfully over and over until you feel deeply that forgiveness in your heart. Nourish yourself with love. Really feel the new, changed you or feel yourself being or receiving what it is you desire.

As an additional healing strand, you might also spread those loving feelings to your present lifetime (and past lives if need be), perhaps imagining each decade as a large box and filling it with a lovely valentine pink color.

While we are inevitably being more loving by merely thinking about it, we can greatly enhance our capacity to express greater depths of unconditional love in the world by feeling it in ourselves first. This working meditation is an excellent place to do that because your connection with your higher self will automatically heighten your experience and comprehension of love, joy, peace and compassion. These higher vibrational energies will thenceforth continue to have striking resonances within your make-up, especially if you can recognize them in yourself each day.

Carry on until troubling emotions, painful memories or current annoyances no longer have any energy or power over you and they have been transformed. You will then reach a place of serenity. This may take several seconds or several minutes. There is no call for turning into a drama queen: you will know in your heart when you have cleared everything you need to for that session. It also bears repeating that you are in a sacred, safe, healing space, so don't worry about incurring bad karma – it won't happen.

Once you have opened your eyes and have recovered your composure, again violet flame yourself and the room as well as any lower vibrational energy you may have released, and express gratitude for the richness of understanding you have gained. Imagine breathing in Light to soothe those bits of you that have let go of old vibrations and are now free to evolve further. Give yourself a hug, and allow yourself and the universe time to adjust to the multilevel healing – this may take a few days. Continue to affirm to yourself the positive messages received at the end of each session until they have been incorporated into your make-up and no longer require your frequent conscious attention.

Repeat the process if necessary: issues can be multifaceted or sometimes behavior patterns have become so entrenched that it takes several attempts to dig them out fully. One way of checking whether they have been completely dislodged and transformed is to go back to words and phrases you have used before – keeping a diary and a note of them can be helpful reminders. If they still have an effect on you, even by a minuscule amount, there is more to be done. It may simply be a case of reminding yourself daily of your empowering message rather than further Word Power work: your heart center will give guidance should you be unsure. If they don't resonate, and you feel perfectly calm and peaceful, then you can move on to the next challenge.

Never pretend to yourself you have dealt fully with your issues if your body and intuition tell you differently. Underlying problems will only surface again at some later stage to hit you in the face.

In summary, Word Power can be broken down into four stages:

(1) *Explain your current situation* in a matter-of-fact way to set the process going, such as:

"I've got a spotty face" or "My life isn't perfect because I'm not spiritual enough."

Repeat this over and over without pausing – except for breath!

(2) *Speak and repeat what you feel physically and emotionally* to take you back to the starting point of your problem, for example:

"My head aches..."
"... aches, aches..."
"I'm fed up..."
"...up, up, up...",
"I'm worthless..."

"I'm not loved by anybody…"
"I DON'T LOVE MYSELF…"

(3) Once you have found the root cause, such as:

"I don't love myself"

follow your inner guidance for healing. Acknowledge the information which has been presented to you, feel it and welcome it – however distressing it may appear – and then allow, for example, unconditional love into your heart.

(4) Finally, *feel what you speak* to reprogram yourself: fully integrate new ways of being, including using positive daily affirmations, such as:

"I love me and God loves me, no matter what."

Chapter 3

More ways to lighten up

When you are experimenting with Word Power, you might try stating the *opposite* of what is going on in your life. Sometimes this can provoke a stronger reaction than describing the actual set-up. So, using a few earlier examples, instead of:

"I'm not vastly wealthy," or
"I don't have loads of friends," or
"I'm not manifesting the best for myself,"

you might say,

"I'm mega rich," or
"I have an abundance of loving friends," or
"I always create what makes me jump up and down with joy."

See what happens for you. As long as you follow your heart, you can sometimes go through an entire series of this sort of positive affirmation in one go to reach your most meaningful code breaker. This is because several spiritual laws are quickly brought into operation simultaneously.

As with any Word Power session, the high frequency energy you generate through your intensely focused intent together with the power of your voice and the healing vibrations of specially-chosen words are like a gigantic vacuum cleaner on a vigorous setting. They draw out, overpower and then convert lower vibrational energy that may have been causing congestion.

Once you access emotions that have been stored in your body, their energy will be released from its cells and tissues. Shedding tears is a good and usually spontaneous way of assisting this. After that there may be nothing more to do. On the other hand, if you have had really deep-seated and longstanding issues, then you may have further experiences to come.

These may take the form of strange aches or odd pains which seem to appear out of the blue. They may occur during or straight after a Word Power session, or they may happen over the next few days. It is certainly something to be aware of because you may inadvertently interfere with the natural process by taking pain killers to dull the "symptoms". I have learned that the longer you ignore them, the more acute they become.

The best way of dealing with any sensation like this is to acknowledge it consciously. Should that fail to improve matters, you may then need to "go into" it. By that I mean concentrate on it and feel it to the core, perhaps bringing in the violet flame too. It may then suddenly intensify – don't be alarmed – before "vaporising" in a succession of bursts, waves or spirals as the energy works its way out. You may have to continue in this fashion for a while until everything has cleared. Soreness afterwards is quite normal, but it usually disappears within a few days as your body sets about repairing itself.

The transmutation process was once quaintly explained to me as being like finding a thread in a knitted item of clothing, and pulling and pulling on it until the garment has been unravelled. The wool can then be washed, maybe dyed (violet-flamed), and reused to create something different, perhaps more stylish. Energy never dies; it is merely altered into a higher or a lower vibrating form.

Analyzing the motives behind your behavior, if you know what they are, and stating these can also reap rewards. It may take courage, especially if you are in the habit of avoiding your truth (many people compartmentalise their life without realising it), but it can be very rewarding in the long run.

Be as specific as you can at the beginning of each session too, as this seems to bump-start the proceedings as well, even if it seems a long sentence, such as:

"I'm frightened of horses because they might kick me," or "Whenever I go to see a movie I feel queasy with the energies there."

You may then find as you carry on that you become less detailed and more global with your descriptions. It is similar to driving a vehicle from cold onto a main road. At the beginning a precise set of procedures has to be gone through, but after that you rapidly gain speed until you have enough momentum to concentrate on the view ahead and forget about how you set off.

On one occasion I wanted to explore why I had so many food sensitivities and decided I would opt for very literal statements about the items I could not tolerate. I used the phrase "I let go of the sensitivity to..." for each of them and, for some bizarre reason, had an acute reaction with "I let go of the sensitivity to garlic." (As far as I'm aware, I'm not a vampire!) As I continued, the focus changed and I found myself facing fears about security and whether it was safe for me as a spiritual being to be in a physical body on earth.

There may be points at which you shift gear on an inner level or enter an altered state of consciousness where you can view yourself from a higher perspective. Here you will access metaphysical truths and gain insights into lessons you are learning. At times you may be acutely aware of the inseparable bond between you and your higher, divine self or you may feel completely at one with All That Is. It is as though a crack into infinity opens up and you glimpse eternal Love – rather like being "in the zone" which athletes describe when they perform at their peak.

On another occasion I was so frustrated at being sick that it seemed I was permanently surrounded by a black cloud. My opening statement then was: "I'm very depressed at always being ill." This soon changed to: "I'm frightened of being well..." and on to: "I fear I may become seriously ill again in the future..."

And after that an even greater leap was made to: "I made other people ill in a past life... I am so sorry... I ask forgiveness of everyone I hurt and I now send love to them via my Higher Self."

After working through each of these stages I could affirm with conviction and sunny optimism: "I am worthy of being well and healthy always."

Such heightened experiences produce intense feelings which will naturally subside until you settle at a new level of awareness. This will not necessarily be of the same vibration as the one you attained during your meditation, but it will be near and it will certainly be beyond your original starting place.

New chakra system

Anyone who is familiar with the chakra system, the energetic equivalent to the human body's nervous system, will probably already have some knowledge of how our thoughts, behavior and attitudes affect each of the cone-like vortexes of energy along our bodies. Chakras which spin sluggishly or excessively fast, or which are blocked, mean that divine life force energy does not flow properly, and this can result in disorders of varying severity.

Should you sense a chakra being brought to your attention during a Word Power session, it may give you a clue as to which associated emotions, patterns or qualities in yourself you might investigate further in a non-judgmental way. Physical sensations, often due to clearing and healing, can sometimes be experienced in one or more chakra areas, traditionally known as the base or root (associated with security and survival), sacral (sexuality and emotional maturity), solar plexus (power), heart (unconditional love and abundance), throat (communication), third eye (inner vision) and crown (connection with the divine).

If you find this happening to you, the following gives very basic, greatly simplified guidance on possible links you might think about (it is a huge area of study and there are many websites and books on the subject):

Chakra	Behavior for slow spin/block	Behavior for fast spin
Root	Lack of confidence	Egotism
Sacral	Hidden emotions, shy	Emotional outbursts
Solar plexus	Self-doubt	Perfectionism
Heart	Lack of self-worth	Domineering
Throat	Timidity	Self-importance
Third eye	Low self-esteem	Arrogance
Crown	Frustration	Emptiness

Comparing other people's interpretations of likely causes of imbalances with your own can be useful in highlighting areas you have not already considered – or in confirming those you are currently exploring, which can be a huge boost to morale. Having said that, you don't have to have any of this information at your fingertips for your Word Power sessions to be successful. Everyone is unique and the source of the dis-ease you are seeking to address may manifest in a slightly different way for you than from that described elsewhere. Feeling chakra movement in these situations simply means that you are on the right track and that restorative action on subtle levels is taking place.

In addition there may be many elements to your "problem" and it will be a case of having to keep digging once you have cleared the more obvious causes. So play around with those phrases of yours and don't give up at the first hurdle. The key is always to describe accurately your up-to-the-minute situation and how you feel about it. Then monitor your body's responses.

It may be an obvious remark to make, but it can get forgotten in the midst of things: always be kind to yourself. Once you are used to tuning in and know yourself very well, you might benefit from a series of short Word Power sessions over a number of days rather than one long session in one day. This may give you the time you and your body need in which to adjust, absorb what you have learned, and allow the next bubble to rise to the surface.

Trust the process: now you have demonstrated your intent to heal yourself, your higher self will be guiding you enthusiastically. As you make progress, shifts may become subtler than they were when you first started out, because the energy you are dealing with will be less and less dense.

Bear in mind too that by incorporating more and more spiritual practices into your life and generally raising your vibration your divine self will initiate you into what has been termed "the light expansion process".

It is a most remarkable phenomenon which allows celestial energies, bringing special qualities appropriate for the next phase of your spiritual journey, to enter, merge with and enhance your chakras. The effect is dramatic, causing existing secondary chakra centers in your hands, knees and feet to be upgraded to primary centers and, through a 180 degree flip, the actual repositioning of chakra energies within your system!

The light expansion process does not happen overnight, and may take many months, perhaps years, depending on each person's ability to handle and integrate the dynamic energies. It is a divine blessing which equips us with vibrant tools and, although you may not necessarily realize it is happening, being aware of its existence can assist you with chakra-based work. This is because some of the emotional roots you are searching for may be quite different from those linked with the "old" chakra system.

In brief, the new chakra positions and the higher qualities associated with each of them are as follows:

Feet – expressing your divinity to the world (walking your talk).

42

Knees – humility, devotion and service to others.

Hands – loving communication of all kinds, including non-verbal methods.

Base of the spine (extending round the hips and lower abdomen) – living and responding always from the heart center.

Mid to lower abdomen – handing yourself over completely to God and co-creating through divine will.

Solar plexus – achieving balance between your physical and spiritual lives, and transformation of old belief systems.

Heart – making the daily choices that cause your heart to sing.

Throat – speaking peace by allowing love to shine through your words.

Third eye – balance and harmony within yourself.

Crown – maintaining a clear dialogue and connection with your Creator at all times.

Of course eventually we will each have one enormous, unified chakra, but until then we can keep our current chakras as healthy as possible. You might use the above as a checklist to help you in your spiritual diagnoses. (There are more details about the light expansion process in *Are you a Master of Light?* – see Books and websites.)

Chakra balancing

However much or little attention you like to pay your chakras, you can always benefit from including in a Word Power session the all-encompassing phrase:

"Through my Higher Self I now cleanse, balance and align my chakras."

Or you could take each chakra one at a time, saying several times over:

"… I now balance my 'x' chakra."

With practice you can do this quite quickly. It can be very useful if, say, you have had an exceptionally hectic morning or a difficult meeting, are frazzled, and wish to regain your composure. With the right intent, it need take only a few seconds of repetitions. It really then is a case of keeping up a light maintenance, checking in from time to time to make sure everything is still clear and balanced.

As part of a regular chakra health check, you might also invoke the violet flame either for each in turn or for all of them together. As you are doing this, you might scan your chakras: use whichever sense comes naturally to you. On occasion you may be shown something that is relevant to your healing.

This next anecdote illustrates the point well. Late one evening Helen tuned in to her chakras, fully expecting them to be in perfect working order. But as she moved to her sacral area there, hovering above, was the symbol of a cross. It did not make much sense to her. Nevertheless the very next day, after a good night's sleep, she twigged. The sign was pointing to the fact that, even though anger had always been quite an alien emotion for her, she was actually holding on to rather a lot of it.

She used to believe it was wrong to show anything vaguely resembling a heated temper, since she thought it would make her a "bad" person. If a situation ever became acrimonious she would usually walk away from it quickly, but if that were not possible she would mentally and emotionally wobble around like a jelly, the tell-tale quaver in her voice being the only noticeable outward sign of inner commotion. Not knowing what else to do, mild irritation, severe annoyance and out and out fury were pushed internally deep down.

She found it rather amusing that the universe had seen fit to direct her attention to a personality trait she had been rather proud of. Friends of a more hot-headed nature than she was would often praise her for being "calm" and "balanced", but all she was really doing was avoiding issues. After being presented with a sign whose name sounds like the very emotion she was running away from, she began to see that there was much indeed within her that was "cross". The spiritual prompt was a timely reminder for her to learn how to deal with it.

Subtle bodies

The same approaches can be adopted for the subtle bodies that comprise our energy field and whose degree of clarity impacts on our health and wellbeing. They have specific functions and vibrate at increasingly higher levels according to their position within the field.

Some people describe large numbers of these components, but it may be simpler to think in terms of three (or four if you count the physical body – it too, of course, is energy): mental, emotional and spiritual, including the etheric which contains the blue print for the physical body (the blue print may be being distorted as a result of energetic blockages).

Once again the aim is to achieve harmony, through releasing any inappropriate energetic clusters that may be muting the efficiency of the subtle bodies. Like the physical vessel, they need to be as clear as possible. A suitable affirmation to adopt for Word Power is:

"Through my Higher Self I now heal and balance my body, mind, emotions and spirit,"

or, as with the chakras, you can take each separately. I have often experimented with this technique and have found it especially helpful to invoke the violet flame again beforehand. The first time I tried: "With the Violet Flame and through All that I AM I now purify my mental body," I immediately experienced a noticeable release of energy from my back, at around heart chakra level.

Another reason for including the subtle bodies in your Word Power affirmation – even though it can sound long-winded – is that their combined energetic strength may help pinpoint the aspect of you that is still hanging onto something the rest of you is keen to relinquish. For instance, you might say:

"My mind, body, spirit and emotions let go of my fear of meeting people."

The phrase is like a massive wide-ranging searchlight sweeping great swathes of countryside at night, and highlighting a small fugitive skulking in the bushes.

To use another analogy, the whole sentence acts like a musical chord. The more notes – key words – there are in the chord, the greater the chance that one of them will vibrate at a frequency which matches, or triggers the emergence of, a subtle blockage.

These blockages are sometimes described as ego-related issues (more about ego in Chapter 5). For instance, you might see a friend's shiny new car and feel a slight twinge of envy, even though you do not consciously want a different car yourself.

Such "negative" emotions can usually be traced back to an insufficiency of some kind, maybe not loving or forgiving yourself enough, not appreciating how masterful a being you are or not fully grasping how much you are loved by others, including Mother/Father God. Many of us know these things already but, perhaps if we were completely honest with ourselves, we tend to forget them from time to time.

Past lives

I had immense fun one afternoon after I hit upon the idea of playing with Word Power to see if I was still holding on to residues from past lives – or what may be perceived as past lives: some people interpret memories, flashbacks or flashforwards as energetic resonances of experiences, past, present and future, held by humanity's group consciousness.

Using the phrase "Through All that I AM I now let go of my 'x' incarnation," I relaxed my mind and asked that, if appropriate and for my highest good, appropriate energies from relevant lifetimes be presented for transmutation.

I was amazed at how quickly a one- or two-word description repeated several times for each, such as "Japanese", "Indian", "Venetian", was forthcoming and at how swiftly I could move from one to the next because energy surfaced so rapidly to be dealt with by the violet flame. There was little need to dwell very long on any of them.

Two, however, did make me pause for a few seconds longer than the others: "Chinese" provoked a very marked reaction, but the most dramatic and unexpected one of all was "Crimean War". A burst of energy shot along the length of my spine like a mini whirlwind. Not being historically inclined, my scant knowledge of the Crimean War could be scrawled on the back of a postage stamp, so it was a surprise to say the least.

Having said that, I recall a battle scene in a dream when I was three or four in which a soldier, wearing a distinctive coat which hung off his shoulder, ran me through with his sword. He was astride a rearing stallion, while I was struggling to defend myself on the ground. I could feel the sensation of the blade as it pierced my flesh. In retrospect, then, perhaps this traumatic incident took place at the end of one of my former lives as a fighting man and reverberations were being brought forward for healing.

It was a very interesting exercise and one you might like to try for yourself. You do not have to go into details for each past life because you are taking a broad-brush approach here to sweep away cobwebs. But if you feel intuitively that a specific lifetime warrants more consideration, then you could choose to probe further. If you do, I would still recommend steering clear of too many particulars: if you become immersed in minutiae, you may lose sight – and feeling – of the larger picture. We are usually only given access to past lives when healing is required, so rather than concentrating on the dress, shoes or food in a period or place, focus instead on the issues producing the blockage and on how to resolve them.

As already intimated, past lives may crop up naturally anyway during the course of other Word Power activity. If this is the case, follow the same principles. An episode I remember vividly involved a lifetime I could place neither historically nor, apart from it being hot and dry, geographically, but in which I felt useless because I was mentally and physically disabled. All I could do was fashion odd pots out of clay, and I hated them because in my eyes people poured scorn on me for them being so misshapen and worthless. In turn I loathed with a passion the folk who apparently despised me.

As the session progressed I realized that, as we have all played the roles of victim and aggressor at some point, perhaps I had made someone else poor in a previous lifetime and that my relationships with the pot-scorning individuals were chosen specially by my soul for my development. I therefore brought forgiveness into my heart and sent it to everyone I thought had hurt me. Within a few seconds in my mind's eye I was completely surrounded by a crowd of people, each of whom was holding a piece of my distinctive lopsided pottery.

I was so touched by this gesture, and even more moved by the sincere message passed on to me: "What you taught us – symbolized by these pots – was important to us. You are worthy, you are loved..." Tears flowed as we all gathered close together for a fantastic group hug.

Another past life was gleaned for me by a clairvoyant. She was given the impression that I served a sentence in a debtors' prison where, because conditions were desperately insanitary, I stopped eating so that my body would not add to the filth in the cell. She then proceeded to "clear" this past life for me, and suggested that it would no longer create food problems for me. "Good," I thought, "that's something I won't have to deal with any more..."

Two years later, however, at about midday I was deliberating over the same old limited options for lunch, trying to find an exceptionally nice snack my insides would tolerate. My intention was that it should be nurturing for my body. As soon as the word "nurturing" came into my mind I sensed a vibration in my lower abdomen.

Having by now used Word Power extensively, I knew straight away that this was a message to indicate an energy session was called for and the sooner the better. So I slipped into an empty room, began Word Power and – bang – there I was in jail, sitting huddled against a damp, crumbling wall, disgusted by my physical form and its functions, and starving myself to death.

There followed one of the most intense emotional outpourings I have ever experienced. I sobbed from what seemed like the depth of my soul, and gasped for oxygen as my lungs were emptied of air while revelation succeeded revelation. Eventually, after forgiving myself repeatedly for how I had treated my blessed body, I opened to a fountain of divine love which washed my grief away.

I have naturally wondered about this significant healing session and the clairvoyant's earlier and, as it turned out, apparently insufficient intervention. I am by nature a skeptic and, because I had not come across anything myself to verify her version of the story, had silently questioned her. Perhaps that negated the effects of her clearing. Or perhaps lack of discernment and an observed tendency in me to be a little slow on the uptake kept me from following up her very helpful lead. Or maybe, continuing the theme of this lifetime's education, I had to do it myself rather than empowering someone else to do it for me.

And the reason a connection with that past life appeared as though out of nowhere? I asked for guidance about this, putting the question: "How does healing come through using Word Power?" The answer was quite straightforward and the analogy like an old spiritual friend:

"Healing is something that will happen for anyone if they are willing to let it into their lives. You already know Word Power is a link between your spiritual godself and your earthly body. You are setting in motion a chain of events that is like a row of dominoes. You spend a long time searching for the beginning of the row – working on yourself – and then suddenly one day you bump into it unexpectedly and the whole row topples over. What delight and what fun!... When your higher and lower minds work in tandem, much can be achieved."

The Karmic Board

It is commonly held today that spiritual seekers have been given a special divine dispensation which allows their karmic slate to be wiped clean. Not long after I became interested in spirituality I, like many people, asked that this should happen, and from then on assumed I would have nothing else to do with the Lords of Karma. This turned out not to be the case.

One afternoon I returned to the question of "confidence", something I always lacked inwardly even if outside appearances suggested otherwise. Using Word Power I tracked back down several routes, but each was met by what felt like a brick wall. The only snippet I could glean was that I believed it was "wrong" to access all my power and so I was functioning on an under-charged battery. Then, as though out of nothingness, came the idea it might be a karmic issue I was coming up against.

I had never considered the possibility before. I had read in total probably only a few paragraphs about the Karmic Board and, apart from the special dispensation, did not know much about it, not even names of members (who change periodically). Nevertheless, trusting this inner voice I began to formulate a request for absolution. Before I had even completed the sentence a deep violet pulsated very brightly on my inner vision, and the flood gates were opened. It was as though I had been given the green light to release a mass of stored energy.

At that instant I somehow knew that during my incarnations on earth I, like most people, have perpetrated the full spectrum of atrocious crimes, although I could not identify any of them individually. Instead, through the tears loomed the figure of a human being in such deep shadow that he/she was completely black and featureless. The image represented the sum total of the so-called evil I have ever manifested. Rather than hide in fear from it, I turned towards it, arms outstretched, and started to utter words of forgiveness.

In the next second I was overwhelmed by tremendous compassion for this darkness. It had been neglected for what seemed like hundreds of thousands of years and was now crying out for love, desperate for understanding. I wept for my entire self, the "good", "bad" and "indifferent", realizing in my heart that I would not be where I am today without having undergone tough challenges where Light and Love were in short supply. Not only that, the lessons learned had brought great knowledge, and by disregarding them I had been depriving myself of the enormous power that comes with wisdom gained through difficult experiences.

I mention this one-off incident because it may be of value if you are having similar problems accessing an obstinate issue. If you have already tried many avenues with no success, then you might consider calling upon the members of the Karmic Board, asking that if it is in your highest spiritual interests they grant you access to the blockage that is preventing you from moving on. You could say something like:

Through my divine Higher Self and under the Law of Grace, I request insight from the Karmic Board into...(*insert words to sum up your stubborn area*)... as well as help in clearing, healing and balancing myself. I thank the Lords of Karma for their loving assistance.

It may be that on occasion, with the agreement of our higher self and the Lords of Karma and Justice (to whom we are brought before each incarnation to discuss lessons and then again afterwards to explain choices made), we are presented with the chance to make a quantum leap forwards in our understanding by consciously taking part in particular aspects of our own slate-cleaning.

It is also worth remembering that the clearing or lightening of ourselves that we undertake can be on behalf of generations who have gone before us. It can be on behalf of humanity currently on earth too. These are service roles we may not necessarily be aware of but to which we committed ourselves before we took on our physical form this time around.

If you feel this may apply to you, treat yourself kindly, ask for as much help as you wish, and know that your endeavours are not going unnoticed by those in the spiritual realms. You will always be supported and the more you can surrender to your divine self, the easier and more rewarding your vocation will be.

However, and this is a big however if you have not done it recently, I would recommend you seek higher guidance for an up-to-date clarification and confirmation of your role. Times are changing and it is no longer necessary for large numbers of us to evolve spiritually through sacrificing ourselves in suffering for others.

On a related note, if you feel you are carrying karma around which you suppose may be someone else's and you do not believe it is your responsibility to transmute it, then the ceremony in Chapter 9 may be helpful.

Tropical moments
The violet energy seen during the karmic episode described in

the last section prompts me to mention another spiritual phenomenon you can use to your advantage. Light from Source is continually beaming down to earth and is comprised of different colored rays, each carrying the resonance of a celestial quality, such as clarity (aquamarine), eternal peace (gold) and divine will (blue).

These rays are often transmitted in pulses and at certain times one may be more dominant than the others as its tempo is quickened and/or its potency turned up several degrees. It is more than likely that, because of humanity's evolutionary next steps, the most active ray overall at the moment is the transformational violet one.

Most people have until now been unaware of the heavenly input we are receiving on a daily basis. But these days, more and more individuals, men and women, are experiencing firsthand "symptoms" that are more usually associated with the female menopause than with spiritual development, such as a sudden rush of heat from head to toe and night sweats.

They are nothing to fear or endure stoically, but are actually to be welcomed, as they signify additional backroom activity on our behalf. The main alchemical element of them all is an extra concentrated dose of the violet flame which burns through layers of dense energy emanating from traumatic events, careless thoughts, so-called ego-led actions and unprocessed emotions. It is quite extraordinary at just how quickly it can be felt in response to even momentary lower vibrational thoughts.

One evening Phil had a quarter of an hour to fill before the start of a program he wanted to watch on television, so he closed his eyes for a catnap. Almost immediately a bright violet pinprick of color appeared. It then grew in size and intensity for a few seconds before the familiar surge of heat coursed through his body.

These tropical or Metatron moments as a friend and I mischievously call them (Archangel Metatron is currently playing a major role in helping humankind raise its vibration) may be accompanied by a sense of unease. That night was no exception, but rather than waiting for it to pass Phil went into Word Power mode to source the weird feelings.

This prolonged the violet and the fierce heat, which was a little uncomfortable, but he soon realized why when long forgotten images from childhood surfaced. His inner child was still being frightened by incidents his adult self had tossed to one side. As part of the healing process he gave his inner child some coping strategies and a big hug, and told him he is always loved. The hotness dissipated straight away, and the pictures and upset were gone.

Should you experience Metatron moments, take a note of what and how you are feeling when they hit – it can be most revealing. Long nights, as opposed to short bursts, of deep frying can be a potential nuisance, but the relief of then being able to unscramble the effects of traumas as they rise up to enter your waking consciousness over the following day or two more than compensates for them.

If you are used to large doses of the violet flame and you are with other people when an energy influx happens, it may be for someone else's benefit and not directly for you: you are merely acting as a transmitter and all you have to do is move fully into your heart center to maximize the effects. This was made evident to Juliet during a visit to one of her acquaintances.

After her arrival they sat down to enjoy a spot of chit chat, and it was not long before Juliet had warmed up so much that she had to take her jacket off. As she fanned her face she made a joke about the tropical moment, although inwardly she was thinking about its unfortunate timing and how she didn't need this right now. Then, a split second later, it was as though her friend was given a cue to unburden herself of a host of family worries.

Although they did not know each other particularly well and had never ventured too far into each other's private life, the woman quite uncharacteristically blurted out major concerns for a relative who was going through a very tough time indeed. In hindsight Juliet felt that the violet flame in this instance had had an enormous effect tangentially.

Ice cool

There may be times when, for no apparent reason, you are anything but hot. In fact however many layers of clothing you put on, you may still feel as though you are sitting on an iceberg. This can also be due to spiritual input from other dimensions. The presence of some cosmic beings can be presaged by penetrating cold, and healing energy can also be cool as well as warm.

In the days before explosives were widely available, rocks would be heated up before being doused with cold water, which caused them to fracture. The beautiful minerals inside could then be more easily accessed. Perhaps we need such treatment in order to shed some of our harder layers. As a monk in a television documentary put it so eloquently, "Blessed are the cracked, for they let in the Light!"

Psychic attachments

There have been times on my spiritual path when, even though other people I trust implicitly have discerned as truth an event they have witnessed, I have been unable to suspend disbelief because I have not experienced it myself. The question of psychic attachments is a case in point.

On a healing course I attended we were asked to scan people's bodies for anything out of the ordinary. There was nothing untoward I could detect, so I was bewildered and somewhat disconcerted when members of the group commented about certain individuals having strangely-shaped spiritual energies and unpleasant-looking beings hooked into them.

The descriptions they gave were of parasitic-type creatures

clinging to hosts. What was most perturbing was that several of my friends saw such beasties on me, around my solar plexus region. By the end of the day I was reassured that they had been removed and that it was nothing to worry or be ashamed about because it was such a common phenomenon.

I was not convinced. If I were honest, I found the whole incident distasteful and abhorred the idea of some awful entities I was unaware of latching themselves on to me and feeding off me. I decided they were not part of my reality and therefore did not exist.

Several years later, I was resting quietly and became aware of pulses of lovely violet. At first I thought they were connected to the physical healing I was by then able to facilitate for myself. But as they grew in brilliance I knew to expect a happening of another sort.

Inner guidance directed me once more to food intolerances and my struggling immune system. Although my overall condition had improved enormously, I was still having bouts of weakness, so I figured I had not ticked off all of the emotional causes to my problems.

I tried to pinpoint when exactly in childhood the sensitivities began. I arrived at a very tender age when I had vivid nightmares in which I dreamed I woke in the middle of the night to the frightening experience of someone, I imagined a man, abusing me. Their heavy, noisy breath on the back of my neck was ferociously hot, but I was too terrified to turn round to see who it was. Even though I was already asleep, the only way I could deal with the situation was to blank it out by getting "back to sleep" as quickly as possible.

I assumed that past life echoes had been replayed through these recurring nightmares – I was far too young to have invented scenarios with such adult themes – and the question was how I should deal with the emotions again presenting themselves. And in that respect I was rather frustrated, because before I embarked on an overtly spiritual journey I worked very hard at dealing with anger and outrage at having been violated early on, even if it were in some other lifetime. I eventually found forgiveness in my heart and reached a state of calm acceptance in which the incidents had no resonance with me. I naturally thought therefore that I had effected all the healing I required.

The violet that day continued to beam down, so it was obvious there was more ferreting around for me to do. Something was outstanding, and I had to find out what. Allowing my higher mind to throw me some clues, I realized that when I first addressed these dreams I knew very little about spiritual matters and had only considered the impact on me personally. I had not considered wider karmic implications. From my clearer vantage point I rapidly grasped that if this had happened to me, then presumably I had similarly imposed my will on others previously.

In that instant of self-recognition the abusing man in my dreams appeared to represent an energetic attachment of those people I had exploited in the past, and was still ignoring. They were literally draining some of my life force away, because I had not acknowledged them or the role I played in our contracted dramas lifetimes ago.

The feeling accompanying this revelation was very different from any other I had experienced before, but I trusted my intuitive interpretation of the situation. It was then that I remembered the gray leech-type beings my friends had caught a glimpse of on the course, and it all made complete sense to me. At that moment I could visualize the entities without disgust.

I recognized their pain and asked their forgiveness, at the same time forgiving myself, and for good measure I requested Archangel Michael to cut cords binding us together. I was left with a sense of completion and love of yet another facet of my being. Quite amazingly, within about a week of this experience, my energy levels started to climb upwards and for the first time in years my immune system kicked in to swamp a virus that in the past would have pulled me down for months.

It might have taken a while for the penny to drop, but it has become evident that we are never victims of such so-called "psychic attachments" or "attacks". Lower vibrational energies are only drawn to us when an aspect of ourselves is unresolved or is in need of healing. There must always be some common thread even if it is a very tiny one, perhaps a shared learning experience, which allows the bond to form and to continue to exist.

Once we own up to it and take steps to transmute it, we immediately radiate Light onto it. Denser energies then will no longer resonate in the same way, and will either leave us or will themselves be transformed. You can help the process along by requesting appropriate healing for them. They are nothing to fear – if as part of your ongoing appraisals of yourself you view them as fragments of you (which technically they are, as we are all part of the same whole), it is easy to surround them with love and hand them over to Mother/Father God.

If you have read this and are now panicking about bugs crawling over you, stop! I have included this section merely for you to be aware of the possibility should similar circumstances crop up in your own healing work. I suggest you call upon your higher self to make known to you whether psychic attachments (or however you wish to view them or name them) are affecting you and, if so, to help you deal with them quickly, sensitively and effortlessly.

For instance, after you have reached a position of understanding between you, and there are no longer any common resonances which might encourage these energies to stay, you could ask angels to accompany them to the Light. The likelihood is, however, that you won't encounter these energetic subtleties unless they are a lesson in your own spiritual education.

Love your body

Another way of accessing your body's codes is to envelop with love aches, pains and ailments, even odd spots and such like, which are trying to attract your attention.

Lie or sit quietly and still your mind. Then say to yourself "I now heal my x," while at the same time imagine flooding the area in question with valentine pink. Take your consciousness or thought into the heart of it. As you merge with and in effect become it, sometimes it will unburden itself straight away. If not, ask why it is unhappy or what message it has for you, and listen to its voice or feel its response.

It often seems as though each organ, muscle, limb etc has its own innate wisdom which can reveal to you what has happened to unbalance it or allowed it to manifest a problem. It can also tell you what you need to do to restore balance. In "reverse therapy", an elegantly simple but dynamic healing system devised by Dr John Eaton, this ability of what he terms the "bodymind" to draw attention through physical symptoms to unprocessed emotions and "headmind's" insecurities is utilized to remarkable effect.

Whenever symptoms flare up a course of action is implemented, including the reading aloud of carefully prepared messages whose words have special, powerful resonance for the individual concerned. This serves to show bodymind that problems are being addressed, and ultimately results in reprogramming of the system, thereby obviating the need for the body to produce any more symptoms. For anyone with an auto-immune problem, including chronic fatigue syndrome, fybromyalgia and food intolerances, or with other conditions such as depression and post-traumatic stress disorder, reverse therapy is certainly worth exploring (see Books and websites).

For some absurd reason I was drawn to use the "love your body" technique on my eyes. Even though my eyelids were shut, I placed a hand over my right eye and concentrated on the left.

The pictures that formed in my mind were attractive and wholesome.

I next turned my attention to the right eye. The scene which materialized for that was, in great contrast, disturbing to say the least. It was dominated by a projectile, maybe a weapon, shooting towards me and then right through my eyeball. On a subtle level I could feel the thud of the impact, but rather than dwelling on it I straight away forgave whoever had initiated the attack, and also myself for similar misdemeanours. The images promptly changed to vignettes of peaceful countryside, so I figured that whatever had needed to be cleared had been.

I have to confess that I was rather dubious about the whole experience. But within about three or four seconds of opening my eyes, a stabbing pain emerged from deep inside my head, at about the position of what I took to be the back of my right eyeball. Energy was then expelled in a few short bursts and before each discharge I could literally feel cells releasing heavy, dense energy. I was left in no doubt about the efficacy of this healing technique, and have used it many times since.

A similar but less involved technique requires you merely to focus on areas of tension. Concentrate on a muscle, group of muscles, a hand or a foot, and think about relaxing them. After a few seconds you may find they want to contract again.

The knack is to counter that natural reaction by commanding them in your mind to relax, relax, relax – and to feel this ease constantly. Gradually the tension will disappear as will the impulse to contract. The more you do this, the more the pattern for tension will be unlearned and your body will obviously be much happier.

I seem to recall a local osteopath telling me that the psoas muscle in particular, a large complicated structure which affects the lower back and hips (and indirectly the legs), can hold large amounts of fear, sometimes stemming from infancy. Having gone through some horrid manipulation to rectify a shortening psoas,

I agree with her that we should not ignore vague stiffness!

Sometimes we do not even know our bodies are not functioning properly because we have become so accustomed to their adaptations. Their love for us is boundless and they will continue to function as best they can for a long time before complaining, if need be absorbing and coping with all manner of onslaughts.

In recognition of their devotion to us, my dear friend Louise created a perfect affirmation which we would like to share with you:

I love my body, my body loves me.
We work together in perfect health and harmony.

Use it each day as a form of gratitude for your unique gift from the Creator, and as a means of honoring your exquisite incarnated self.

Chapter 4

Self-attunements for healing

You may feel great anticipation when you set about a new attunement. A sense of adventure often kicks in because you can never be completely certain where you will be led, who you will meet or what you will end up doing. There is no doubt about it: these ceremonies can be quite magical. Although they are not essential for spiritual development, they do seem to precipitate growth, sometimes in great spurts.

They are a sacred ritual of your own making, so they can help you assert yourself and take positive action at critical moments in your life, such as when you have reached a cross-roads or an especially low (or high!) point. All in all, they can be both stimulating and incredibly productive.

This chapter contains ideas for multi-strand healing through a graded series of personal attunements, from opening your healing channels to healing at soul level. Each has been blessed by the ascended realms so that you will receive whatever is most appropriate for you and at the highest vibration.

Assuming you are content with the ideas, start with whichever attunement resonates with you the most and leave the rest for the time being. You can return to others once you have had a chance to think about them some more.

The wording printed here is not set in stone, but is merely a series of guidelines. You may choose to use it as it stands or you may wish to adapt it to reflect your needs, beliefs and desired outcomes. Alternatively you may prefer to devise your own wording that represents you more accurately and what it is you are seeking.

Whether you opt for some of these attunements or you strike

out on your own, be prepared for the odd marvel or two around the corner – always expect the unexpected! If you trust that anything is possible through love, you open yourself up to wonderful surprises. I have included some personal stories for background color, and also to illustrate what can be achieved through the most rudimentary of ceremonies and the simplest of wording. Your own experiences, of course, may be quite different, but they will be equally precious and perfect just for you nevertheless.

God's Gift: Opening to heal

This first attunement was designed mainly to facilitate the start of "hands-on healing" during which, in basic terms, spiritual healing energy flows through the crown chakra and then on down through the arms and out through the hands of the healer. In other words the ceremony reconnects and opens your spiritual channels in the most appropriate way for you so that you can access additional healing energy from Source via your higher self.

We are each born with a gift of healing: it is not special to a few individuals, but is merely an extenuation of our natural reaction to reach out to someone to comfort them when they are in distress – the best tonic in the world can be as simple as a warm smile, a touch of the hand or a big hug. But sometimes accessing, even recognizing, our deep healing ability takes time and, quite often, confidence.

In the case of spiritual healing, conducting a ceremony can help here. However formal or informal you make it, the ritual creates a heightened sense of purpose but also in a curious way takes some of the pressure off you. Whilst you are being as proactive as you can to change your circumstances, you also allow yourself to let go of your inhibitions and become the healer that God intends. Concern about how this is brought about by the spiritual dimensions evaporates as you surrender to the process. In essence you are learning to believe in yourself and in your divine guidance.

Personal opening

Thanks be to God for Power, Love, Light, Energy and Healing. (x3)

I AM a Master of Light. I call to me the Presence of my Higher Self. (x3)

Through Divine Light and Grace and in the name of All that is Love, through the Presence of my Higher Self, I call upon Archangel Raphael, Archangel Michael, Archangel Sandalphon, ascended masters Hilarion, Quan Yin, St Germain, El Morya... my healing guides and any other cosmic being of Love and Light who is meant to be present now and is willing to assist me with the opening of my healing channels. (x3)

I AM a Master of Light. Through my Higher Self I invoke the Violet Flame to transmute energy in and around me, and transform it into Light. (x3)

I AM a Master of Love and Light. Through my Higher Self I ask that I be opened to channel healing energy – whatever is appropriate and for my highest good – NOW. (x3)

(Imagine a golden beam of Light from the Source of all healing entering through the top of your head and linking with your heart center in the middle of your chest. Take it down through your body, through your feet into the depths of Mother Earth and up again to your heart center. Then take it out to the tips of your fingers on your right hand, back across your chest, out to the fingers of your left hand, and return to your heart center. Do this twice more, each time broadening the beam of Light until you are fully eveloped by it and you feel as though it is permeating your entire body, right down to a cellular level. You are now vibrating to your own personal healing frequency of Light and Love.)

I AM a Master of Light. Through my Higher Self I thank all beings present for helping me and ask that they continue to guide me so that I may use my healing gift with discernment and wisdom for the benefit of myself and everyone I come into contact with. (x3)

I AM a Master of Light. Dear God, I thank you. (x3)

Thank you. So be it. So it is.

Once you are connected to healing energy, simply allow it to flow. You might start off by saying to yourself, "I now allow healing energy to flow freely through my hands." Spend time practicing with it, getting to know how it affects your body first before offering to try it out on friends and family. Read about how other practitioners approach the subject of hands-on healing, and then form your own opinion about what is right for you. You may be drawn to join a group of like-minded people, or you may prefer to develop on your own.

If someone who appears to have more experience than you recommends a particular technique or way of doing something, this does not mean you have to adopt their methods. Discern what is your own healing path, even if it apparently contradicts every one else's. Maybe you are meant to manifest your gift in a totally different way in order to bring a wider perspective to the healing fraternity or to introduce new ideas that are relevant for humankind's ongoing evolution.

A quick trawl on the internet recently threw up literally hundreds of healing methods involving spiritual energy. On reflection this seems most apt. As skilful divine beings we each have a wealth of unique experiences and preferences which shape who we are. It is therefore possible that a healing modality tailor-made to our distinct specifications may allow us to express our talents and creativity more fully than one which caters broadly for everyone.

For a comparison think of the fashion industry. However expensive the material from which they are made, off-the-peg clothes do not fit everyone perfectly because differently shaped bodies have curves and bumps in all sorts of places. The best fitting and most attractive garments still tend to be those cut and sewn to accommodate a person's very individual measurements.

I am reminded of a lady I met on a course who sensed that the healing energy with which she was working often seemed to be imbued with the essence of medicinal herbs which varied according to each client's needs. While she is a keen advocate of the benefits of herbalism, she has never felt the need to spend time studying it because she understands intuitively that this was something she accomplished during a past life.

To save herself duplicating effort in this lifetime, she is therefore now accessing that wisdom and using it in a novel way to develop her current healing skills. In effect she is creating her own new "brand" of healing energy that is evolving from the cumulation of her learning experiences. This must be very rewarding: bringing together a number of personal enthusiasms, as well as expertise – past and present, and maybe future – into a rich, eclectic mix.

Use your gift responsibly and honestly, and with humility and gratitude. If you choose to develop it to help others, you may in time find yourself acting as an intermediary. It is a very satisfying role but one not to be undertaken lightly. You will naturally need to research legal, ethical and personal requirements should you wish to practice in the public domain. And you will also have to be clear about your own spiritual responsibilities.

To be of the greatest service the aim is to be as clear a channel as you can be. This will probably involve further personal development work so that you can reach a balanced state of what is often referred to as "detached compassion" or "loving detachment". From this "ego"-less vantage point you do not impose yourself or promise specific outcomes because you know that all is facilitated through God's grace, a client's higher self and their body's own powers of recovery.

Clare, a distant relative of mine via marriage, offered to take the personal opening attunement as part of an experiment for this book, and is happy to share her experiences so far. Her spiritual healing currently seems to be showing itself not so much through the conventional full-on way of channeling energy but as a subtle progression towards wholeness through gentle improvements and personal insights. This is how she explained it to me:

The main thing I noticed… was a gradual feeling of acceptance and peace. Things that would have worried or irritated me didn't seem to matter any more. The best example of this was some haphazard sleeping arrangements during our summer holiday which would usually have made me feel panicky and miserable but which just didn't matter. If things continue in this vein, I might even be able to consider camping one day! Anyway, I have become much more accommodating. I have also felt a strong desire to stop trying to do things that aren't suited to my nature (certain jobs, seeing certain people) and to stop trying to make myself fit in. This is where the sense of acceptance has been strongest.

I have asked for healing to help with specific problems, including stomach pains, which gradually died away over a few hours, returned a couple of days later, then disappeared. I've done the same for general health issues and my younger son's tumor.

If you are drawn to other branches of the healing arts rather than to hands-on healing, such as homeopathy, aromatherapy, reflexology, shiatsu, etc, you can still use the ceremony – with modified wording – to bring you into contact with people and circumstances that will open doors for you.

Or you might ask to be introduced to an unknown (to you and/or to the rest of the world) form of healing which will bring you the job satisfaction you are looking for, perhaps through making this sort of request:

Through God's Love and Grace, and with the guidance and support of my Higher Self and compassionate beings of Love and Light, I now empower myself to access my infinite healing potential and through joy to discover and live my true healing path for this lifetime. May I be shown (new) ways of healing which enable me to use my talents most effectively and which further develop my expression of unconditional love in service to the Creator.

Helper and receiver

I used the following modified version of the personal opening attunement with my husband. This is suitable for situations in which a more experienced healer – although it does not have to be – introduces "novices" to hands-on healing energy. Again, it could be altered for anyone interested in other forms of healing.

Thanks be to God for all Power, all Love, all Light, all Energy, all Healing. (x3)

I AM a Master of Love and Light. I call to me the Presence of my divine Higher Self. (x3)

I AM a Master of Love and Light. Through my Higher Self I call upon (*name's*) Higher Self and ask for your assistance and guidance for whatever is the best for (*name's*) highest spiritual evolution. (x3)

I AM a Master of Love and Light. In the Name of Love, through All that I AM, I call upon the ascended realms, Archangel Raphael, Archangel Michael, Archangel Sandalphon, ascended masters Hilarion, Quan Yin, St Germain, El Morya... and any other other cosmic being of

Light and Love who is meant to be here now and is willing to assist with (*name's*) opening to channel healing energies. (x3)

I AM a Master of Love and Light. Through All that I AM I invoke the Violet Flame to transmute energy in and around (*name*) and me, and transform it into Light. (x3)

I AM a Master of Love and Light. Through Divine Light and within the Law of Grace, I command that (*name*) be opened to channel healing energies – whatever is appropriate and for his/her highest good – NOW. (x3) Thank you.

(Here you might like to draw the infinity sign within a heart three times at the crown, third eye, throat and heart chakras (see the next section for further information about using symbols), and also on or over each hand and foot, while stating aloud or in your head "Let there be Light and Love". At the end you might place your hands on the person's shoulders to make a connection and to acknowledge the healing energies between you. These instructions are merely suggestions – you may prefer an alternative approach.)

I AM a Master of Love and Light. Dear God, I thank you for your precious gift. (x3)

Thank you. So be it. So it is.

For groups

A combination of both versions of this Opening to heal attunement, in which "we" is substituted for "I", has worked well in group settings. Members decide for themselves whether they wish to keep the existing wording or would prefer to change it.

It goes without saying that the loving energy generated by numbers of people gathered together with a common purpose and concentrating on a ceremony they have created between them can be immensely powerful. Blockages that in the past may have been preventing individuals from giving spiritual healing can soon be swept away.

One aspect of group work I have experimented with is to ask each person to contribute a symbol for the occasion. A large clean sheet of paper is placed on the floor and people are invited to sit in a circle around it. They then take it in turns to draw on the paper whatever comes intuitively to mind. Their personal motif is an expression and celebration of their uniqueness and brings a very special element to the attunement. The resulting combination of symbols can then be focused upon during the ceremony, maybe at a point agreed by everyone beforehand.

Symbols

The question of symbols is an interesting one. For some well-known attunements, such as those undertaken by reiki exponents, the drawing and invoking of them form a major part of the proceedings and afterwards in healing sessions. The results of reiki enthusiasts throughout the world speak for themselves and, having used them myself, I am in no doubt that symbols can be extremely efficacious.

I am aware too that when we are periodically "downloaded" with information from the celestial realms we often receive higher spiritual wisdom in the form of codes and mathematical symbols, as well as in the language of light, a high-vibrational method of communication between masters which itself is based on a common system of emblems.

However, my own nature is such that I find having to remember a lot of prescribed details, especially what to use when, is overly complicated for me. I usually function best when I can respond spontaneously, via a connection with my heart center and higher self, to someone's needs without being side-tracked by what can seem like a complicated set of procedures.

I know many people have a different attitude and a greater ability to remember facts and figures than I have, and are drawn to the magic, mystery and potency of symbols. But after some deliberation, my inclination is not to include any specific ones for the attunements here and to leave the choice up to you. (The heart and infinity symbols in the last attunement are not essential, but they often feel appropriate – for me; they may not for you...)

So my recommendation for you is to extemporize. Be creative. Have fun. With guidance from your divine self and spiritual mentors, devise your own symbols or be open to receiving new ones, perhaps in the form of vocal noises or musical notes, because they may be the perfect match you need at that very second for your ceremony: as you progress, what was once appropriate for you, even something you invoked the previous day, may no longer be the best choice. Hush your mind, connect with your heart center and request an image or series of images that are suitable for you. Then draw whatever comes forward.

Alternatively stick with the signs you know and are happy with, but perhaps use them, with due reverence, in a new context. Be unconventional! Adopting that attitude can often yield great insight.

Or you may prefer to leave them out of your ceremony altogether and, by so doing, place no limitations whatsoever on what you receive from Spirit. It really is a matter of how you perceive the nature of symbols and whether your feel they have any relevance for you. There is no right or wrong.

Before I leave the subject for the time being, there is one important aspect of symbols used during any form of ritual which I would like to flag up. And that is their longevity. By this I mean that once they have been introduced into your energy field, they remain there indefinitely, even after they are past their sell-by date. As you evolve, it may no longer be appropriate for you to continue carrying them around with you, but they are still there, blocking your system and in effect preventing you from reaching your full potential.

Therefore, if you do incorporate symbols into your attune-ments, I would advocate including this sort of caveat:

Through Divine Law and Grace, and in the Name of God, through All that I AM I command that the symbols, signs, codes and seals used in this ceremony and placed within my energy field and body be blessed with and by Light and Love; and that they remain activated for as long as they serve my highest interests. (x3)

Once they are no longer of the correct vibration for me, I request that they be raised in vibration in accordance with my current needs. Or, if that is not appropriate for me, may they be removed from my being. Let them then be transmuted by the power of the Violet Flame, transformed into Light and returned to Source. So be it. (x3)

A cleansing exercise you can usefully perform at any time is the removal of energetic carry-overs from sacred-type rituals in this and past (and even future) lives which have become surplus to requirements. These energies are often seen by clairvoyants as symbols and such like within chakras or the subtle bodies. They may be the very signs that were drawn during the original ceremonies, or they may be symbolic representations of oaths or vows.

You may already have been made aware of vows through your current life experiences, in which case the invocations in Chapter 1 and Chapter 8 can be used to address these. Symbols that were drawn or conjured, on the other hand, as opposed to depictions of spoken statements of intent, are a very different kettle of fish. You may have any number of these and it may not be a realistic option to try dealing with each individually. In this case there is no beating about the bush – you need to assert your mastery in order to effect the clearing:

Through Divine Law and Grace, and in the Name of Love, through All that I AM I call upon Archangel Metatron, the angels and archangels of healing, time devas and my spiritual guardians... (x3)

Through Divine Law and Grace, I command that:

all signs, symbols, codes and seals and other manifestations of my sacred commitments and initiations which are within my body and being and which are now outdated, inappropriate or no longer of benefit to my highest good be removed NOW. (x3)

I command under the Law of Grace that they be transmuted by the power of the Violet Flame and Violet Fire, and transformed into Light before being returned to Source. May Light and Love also enfold me for healing. So be it. So it is done. So it is. (x3)

Through my Higher Self I now restore balance to myself, and bless those who have helped in this cleansing. (x3) Namaste.

There can be a great sense of liberation after this decree. I can assure you that you will not lose any of your healing abilities – or any other gifts come to that. In fact you will be a much clearer channel as a result.

Moving on

Manifestation of your desired outcome for each of the attunements in this book, as well as for others you create, will be determined by many factors, including your degree of openness, faith and belief in yourself. Some of these factors may not even have registered in your conscious mind. It will also depend on what is chosen by your higher self to give you the biggest learning opportunities.

The aim of attunements is always to invite the universe to provide you with the absolute best, at the highest vibration possible, via whichever means is most suited to you. This is why some of the invocations and decrees are open-ended – no restrictions are placed on what, how and to a certain extent when you may receive.

Sometimes your healing ceremonies may not bring the results you expect directly to you on the spot but at a later date indirectly. On occasion you may be guided to transmute feelings of unworthiness before you can enjoy fully the abundance you merit as a being of Light. Or you may have to determine whether on some level you are harboring a restricting belief in the need for an intermediary, someone better, more advanced than you in the physical dimension, to conduct attunements on your behalf.

At one extremely challenging point in my life I reached the conclusion that it would take nothing less than a miracle for my body to return to health. As I had already tried innumerable ways to cure myself, each of which was unsuccessful and basically depended on other people to do it for me, I was now forced to delve into my inner resources to find a solution on my own. I put Word Power to the very real test of eradicating from my mind every single fear about my wellbeing I could possibly think of and every limiting belief about "miraculous healing", a phenomenon I believed could occur for others, but not for me.

I cannot recall exactly how long I spent on this exercise, but it can only have been a few sessions. I was extremely determined. What I do remember is the end stage. It was as though I was surging upwards through a dark tunnel, clearing barrier after barrier as I considered every conceivable restricting thought pattern until suddenly the last one was blasted away and a gorgeous pink energy erupted like a volcano onto my inner scene.

I then felt such unconditional Source love and compassion that in those few seconds of rapture I fully comprehended and believed at a profound level that anything is possible: miracles did not just happen to other people – they were to be part of my life too. I could also affirm with complete, immovable conviction "I am worthy of perfect health", a statement so vibrant with divine love due to the experience that even today it still shines like a golden beacon in my life.

This inner work, in which I experienced tangibly my godself – the eternal part of me that does not get bogged down with personality issues – and which established a conscious, continuous connection between higher and lower minds and my body's own innate intelligence, then paved the way for the miracle I so badly wanted to be brought about.

I am reminded of a spiritual conundrum many people will be familiar with. Discerning when to seek and accept assistance, go it alone, or do nothing is not always as straightforward as it might be. In fact it can be very tricky indeed reading a particular set of circumstances, especially when you are banking on something happening and it's just not materializing. This joke says it all.

There once was a man who found himself in a life-threatening predicament but, as a person of faith, he called upon God to rescue him. The first day a neighbor rushes up and throws the man a rope, shouting, "Hold onto the rope and I'll pull you out of trouble."

"No thank you, neighbor," the man says. "God will save me."

The next day a horse walks by and asks the man to climb up on her back so that she can take him to safety. Again, the man declines.

On the third day a gargantuan golden eagle wearing a dazzling golden crown flies overhead and offers to carry the man in his talons to the security of friends.

Yet again, he declares, "No, thank you. God will save me!"

On the fourth day, no one comes to the man's aid, and he is overwhelmed by his plight and dies. After he has passed over, he kneels before God and in a somewhat belligerent tone complains, "What happened God? Why didn't you come and save me?" to which God sighs and replies, "Did I not send you a neighbor, and then a horse who could talk and even after that for goodness

75

sake the largest golden eagle in the world who likes to wear a crown...?"

You might recall this tale the next time you are debating about what to do next or you are tempted to think your attunement has not worked. Keep a watch out for unexpected openings. They may not be immediately obvious, especially if the universe is pulling strings in a way that is strikingly different from what you are accustomed to.

Never dismiss anything without first checking within to find out how the wise inner you feels about it.

Upgrading the system

An attunement you could take on a regular basis involves asking for a boost to your healing gifts – rather like upgrading a computer program. If you feel it is time to re-evaluate your healing and you would like to widen your experience, then I suggest the following. This wording may prompt you to consider what exactly it is you would like for yourself:

> Through Divine Light and Grace and in the Name of Love, I ask that my connection with my Higher Self be strengthened and stabilized, and that my healing abilities be refined, expanded and raised in vibration according to my current stage of spiritual development. May I use my gifts responsibly with wisdom and compassion for the benefit of all beings. (x3)

The more evolved you become, the more subtle opportunities – and challenges – can be. But you may also have to be patient: as mentioned above, your petition will have been noted and will be being acted upon, but your higher self, viewing the situation from a far greater perspective than you presently can, may need to make the sort of adjustments you may not yet be in a position to consider.

If much time goes by and you are still in doubt about your

route forward, spend a few seconds placing one or both hands on your heart center, and affirm to yourself what you are aiming to achieve, such as:

"I now freely access abundant healing energy."

Say this several times, as though you are in Word Power mode, and imagine how you will feel when the target is reached. This action can often uncover emotional blockages requiring removal. It may also confirm or reject your project: when you place yourself in alignment with your higher self through making contact with your heart center, you soon discover whether your lower and higher minds are still working together or against one another. You may have to reappraise your motives as well as your desires.

If after doing this you feel that you may be blocking yourself on a subconscious level which you can't quite grasp, try the following:

Through Grace and under Divine Law I ask that I now be released from (*or* I now release myself from) physical, mental, emotional and spiritual pain, suffering and lack, and that I be healed completely in every particle of my being in all time frames, dimensions and realities. (x3)

I command that any outstanding sabotaging aspects of myself – mental, emotional, physical or spiritual, or any other part of my being – which need to be healed and integrated before I can move to oneness be brought forward quickly, easily and gently. May they be transmuted by the power of the Violet Flame and transformed into Light and Love. (x3)

A general note here about pain, as healing can range from complete cessation of "symptoms" to a serene acceptance of what may appear to be a soul's difficult choice of body. Most of us have experienced pain at one time or another. Some people adopt the role of martyr as a coping strategy, perhaps not paying enough attention to why it is there, accepting it as their fate and trying to ride over the top of it – I know this one well! A lesson may therefore be to learn to let go of the causes of and need for pain, and pain itself, and to understand fully that suffering is not always inevitable or even necessary. It is really what we elect, at some level, for ourselves. As humanity builds a new paradise, many may seek alternative methods of dealing with the ups and downs in life that do not always lead to hurt.

No one of course should be criticized for having pain. There are innumerable reasons it arises, such as adhering to belief systems that have been carried over from past lives, and continually disregarding spiritual laws and warning signs. It may also be used as a substitute for love or as a way of someone grounding themselves into the physical dimension.

Aside from these explanations, there are many enlightened souls out there, including those who have looked at their health problems from every conceivable angle for years, who no matter what they do still find themselves with chronic illness. The mission of these brave individuals may be to draw our attention to the plight of our brothers and sisters on the planet whose lives continue to be marred by the distress of war, an unhealthy environment, abuse, poverty, animosity from neighbors, etc. Serving as humble messengers and immense teachers, they inspire and motivate us all with love to redress global imbalances and to provide help closer to home.

And then there are people who are using their bodies to transmute lower vibrational energy into a higher form. In short, no one can ever truly understand the reasons for someone else's pain, but self-knowledge through connection with higher guidance can certainly bring insight into your own situation and what you need to do for your own healing.

Expanding further

As you progress on your spiritual journey, you may find yourself being encouraged to consider yourself in new, challenging ways. Each of us has energetic components within many dimensions which we can learn to access. By dimension I mean a band of frequencies in which beings or spiritual energies of a certain evolutionary state choose to reside.

Some people deem there to be twelve dimensions, while others believe there are far fewer or many more – it is currently being suggested that as we embark on creating a different way of life for humanity, we are now being permitted access to the thirteenth dimension and beyond.

As I understand it, dimensions do not have a beginning or an end, but blend into one another in the same way that the colors of the rainbow merge and are not really separated from one another. In other words they are merely a human interpretation of a continuum of ever deepening consciousness and unconditional love.

The next healing attunement is what you might call more expansive than the previous ones because in it you acknowledge your multilevel existence and, as a result of that, open yourself up to greater opportunities. You are far more than a human being with spiritual leanings on the earth plane:

Thanks be to the Creator for Compassion, Power, Joy, Love, Life, Energy, Healing. (x3)

I AM my multi-dimensional self. I now call to me my Light of God, my soul, to assist me under the Law of Grace. (x3)

I AM my multi-dimensional self. In the Name of Love, through All that I AM I request the presence and help of:

Lord Sanat Kumara, Lord Venus Kumara, Archangel Metatron, Archangel Gabriel, Archangel Michael, Archangel Raphael, my healing guides and mentors, Master Hilarion, Master Quan Yin, St Germain... and any other ascended cosmic being of Love and Light who wishes to help me now. (x3)

I AM my multi-dimensional self. Through my I AM Presence I invoke the Violet Flame to transmute energy in and around me and transform it into Light. (x3)

I AM my multi-dimensional self. I ask through All that I AM and under the Law of Grace that my body and subtle bodies be attuned to the most powerful and potent spiritual healing energies suitable for me right now. I promise to use my gift with integrity, supporting my body and being and, when appropriate, facilitating for the highest good of others. (x3)

Through All that I AM I give thanks to everyone present who is assisting with this attunement process. Blessings and love to you all. (x3)

Dear Mother/Father God, I thank you from the bottom of my heart. (x3)

While in my meditation after this attunement much physical activity went on in and around me. It seemed that there was a person either side of me, and someone else put their hand on my brow. Rapid eye movement, as information was downloaded, was so fast and furious that my eyelids vibrated like the wings of a hovering insect.

Then followed a calmer period accompanied by a coldness throughout my body and shivers up and down my spine. Several phases of emotional releasing ensued during which a message came into my mind: "there are limitless possibilities – open to them," at which point I asked there and then that my heart and mind be opened to accommodate the new (you might incorporate this request in your own attunement).

Next I felt as though I was being taken through space to another planet where I sat in a crystal chamber. Other beings sat in a circle round the outside, and projected their thoughts and healing energy at the chamber which amplified them for me. Further scenes were played out on my inner visual screen and towards the end white-furred animals and a unicorn appeared.

Once back on earth I sat with faeries, which prompted another bout of crying because I felt sure that I was grieving somehow for their counterparts out in the cosmos whom I sorely missed. I have subsequently and affectionately called them "cosmic faeries". From this rediscovered affinity with these beings, I have deduced that they collaborate with healing energies in the higher dimensions, helping humanity evolve and prepare conditions for a "new earth".

The downloading of information continued for the rest of the afternoon, and on into the evening. At one stage I felt so cold that I put on a dressing gown over the top of my already thick day clothes. Physically and emotionally I was very much at a low ebb, but as I contemplated the day I could not help but marvel at the extraordinary experiences which had been prompted by the ceremony. I went to bed early and slept like the proverbial log, although at times I was aware of intense fifth-dimensional colors and shapes in dreams.

The next morning, as I again reflected on the previous day's events, I was moved to contemplate the vastness of creation. It was also brought home to me again how important it is to recognize that as we grow spiritually we should be aware of possible consequences of our actions. These may propel us into unfamiliar territory which causes us to delve deeper into our being to find out how to navigate through it. This can be both exciting and demanding at the same time.

After a self-attunement we may be hit by a sudden bout of challenges we had not bargained for, but these merely serve as opportunities for us to stabilize our vibrations. This type of spiritual ceremony brings about a raising of our frequency through an influx of information and Light, which in turn highlights anything of a lower vibration in our lives which does not match it.

As spiritual law decrees, higher vibrations attract and transform lower ones. So in order to maintain this elevated level of consciousness (you may choose not to – which is fine, but you may return to your former frequency), fears, emotional blockages, less than favourable behaviors, damaging relationships and the such like which have the potential to pull us down must be healed. Word Power really does come in extremely handy here.

Similarly, if you have already dealt with a particular issue only to find it reappear again after an attunement, don't be dismayed. You may be in touch with the part of its energy which resides at the higher frequency in which you are now operating. This should mean it has less power over you than it did when you first acknowledged it.

Imagine a weed: it has leaves and flowers above ground, and under the soil it has a long carrot-shaped root, stout at the top and tapering to a point with fine hairs and mini-roots at the bottom. Weeds are notoriously difficult to eradicate because their roots extend so far down into the ground.

In a spiritual sense you are like a gardener trying to create a handsome garden full of flowers that are not choked off by weeds (weeds are perfect in their own patch). You sometimes have to dig deep to remove all of the root system – it's easy to leave small pieces behind, but these still have to be reached to prevent any chance of the plant re-establishing itself.

To fulfill your potential then – perhaps to attain that fantastic goal you have set yourself in a ceremony – trust that everything is in perfect celestial order even if at times you wonder what on earth you have let yourself in for. This is not meant to sound like a government health warning. I mention it only as a reminder that the more spiritually mature you are the more you can accomplish if you are prepared to continue revealing more and more of your multi-dimensional self by clearing out the weeds.

And of course I don't need to remind you that the journey is usually much more interesting and intriguing than the destination itself. It is possible to become so bound up with future outcomes that the sheer heavenliness of each day is missed.

Mahatma and more

The sort of healing energy I have worked with on myself for many years usually involves engaging a connection with it through the briefest of thoughts and allowing it to operate (with mind and body assisting where necessary) in whatever way it knows best. I have often referred to some of the accompanying sensations as being like spiritual microsurgery, but the norm is more akin to sharp knives and burning needles of varying diameters.

There have also been times when tremendous electric currents have shot from A to B, presumably along meridian lines acupuncturists are familiar with, and blasted anything in between. (Having innocently had a drink a few seconds after I experienced this phenomenon around my mouth, I am not overstating the electrical component. As I rapidly discovered, water and electricity don't mix!) For a long time I have rarely used my hands for healing. There has simply been no need.

It has always been a robust form of energy to clear physical and energetic blockages, but on one occasion after an attunement its intensity verged on nothing short of ferocious. I was due to visit friends for lunch. During the morning I lay on the bed while a force surged through me like a tornado as it tried to corkscrew up my body, causing me to jerk around quite spectacularly.

It was thrilling to experience, until the moment when a massive involuntary movement caused me to pull a muscle in my neck. After that, much to my friends' amusement, I could barely turn my head left and right. If I was to avoid more tweaked muscles, I was going to have to get the energy toned down, but on the other hand I did not wish to lose its potency.

That evening I came across a couple of paragraphs I had been sent in an e-mail about "the Mahatma energy". From what I could gather it embraces myriad aspects of unconditional love – the pure essence of healing – that is funneled to earth through and by the collective consciousness of the ascended masters.

The higher the dimension and its vibration, the more likely its spiritual consciousness will be of a group nature rather than that of many individuals. To put it another simplistic way, the closer to pure Source you get, the more you lose your sense of "self" and the more you become at one, or indeed one with, the Creator and Creation.

Bearing this in mind and the fact that "Mahatma" is the sanskrit word for "great soul", you might see the Mahatma energy as an invitation to acknowledge more fully your association with the rest of the cosmos via your divine self.

Before retiring for the night, I touched base with my heart center and invoked the Mahatma energy. Astonishingly there was an immediate calming of the healing roar. In spite of this dramatic effect, I was left with the distinct impression I was missing a piece of the jigsaw puzzle.

I quizzed my higher self about this and received greater clarity about a subject I had been introduced to earlier via the unloved, shadowy "evil" figure mentioned in the previous chapter. To recap, in order to manifest everything that brings us happiness and contentment, we need to welcome and love absolutely those energies we generated during past lives and in other dimensions which, because they may be unpleasant reminders of personal actions we would rather forget about, we may have turned our backs on.

Even if we consciously cut ties to previous traumatic events or to a specific past life because we believe they have been having a "negative" effect on us, we still own and have responsibility for the energy left behind. Although perhaps now scattered and fragmented, it will not be fully transmuted until we have taken ownership of it (just as we are learning to accept all aspects of our personality in this lifetime) and then either reintegrated it or returned it to Source.

The possibility of a new ceremony for what might be called a multi-dimensional spiritual spring clean suddenly became very attractive. Three immediate benefits were stressed, once again following principles outlined previously.

One: by accepting those aspects of ourselves which, through their courageous choices, helped us learn about Light and absence of Light we can grow through developing greater compassion for ourselves.

Two: this process allows us to claim back for ourselves in full the power, wisdom, understanding and strength we gained during those challenging times but which we later neglected through fear of embracing the "dark".

And three: by transmuting lower vibrational energy that has been holding us back, we are free to move on unencumbered.

A buzz of excitement hummed through me as I put pen to paper for this attunement. I felt sheer joy at the prospect of what I was about to undertake and afterwards was left with a deep sense of peace. Although I had probably only touched the tip of the iceberg as far as the Mahatma energy was concerned, I did now have a firmer grasp of its potential to bring about change through motivating us to look through a wide-angled lens at ourselves.

Here is the multi-dimensional "spring clean":

I hereby acknowledge and accept full responsibility for each part of my being, everything that I have ever done and will do, and everything that I have experienced and ever will. (x3)

Through my I AM Presence, under the Law of Grace and in the Name of God, I decree that disparate energies of mine from the past, present and future in this and every alternative reality and dimension be transmuted through the power of the Violet Flame and Violet Fire into Light and Love. (x3)

Through my I AM Presence, under the Law of Grace and in the Name of God, I decree that those energies serving my highest good now be integrated and aligned within my being for completeness and perfection of All that I AM, and that other energies which I no longer need be returned to Source. May all be brought into perfect balance and harmony. (x3)

Through my I AM Presence, under the Law of Grace and in the Name of God, I ask that my body and subtle bodies be attuned to as much and as many complexions of the Mahatma energy as is appropriate for me at this time, and that I have continual easy facilitation of Love's healing for the benefit and highest good of everyone. (x3)

I now embrace and acknowledge the full power of my being. (x3)

Multi-dimensional healing attunement

The next attunement may appear similar but is actually subtly different and is a natural follow-on to the previous one. A lot of us probably spend much of our time focusing on what you might call our immediate self – our mind, body and emotions and our higher or spiritual part closest to us – but as our being is vast and spans the entire spectrum of consciousness, we have in a sense many higher selves in different dimensions.

If you take the analogy of a ladder to represent our spiritual progress in raising our vibration, each rung above us is like a higher self. It always vibrates faster than that of our current position until we reach its level and it is then integrated. This means we always have an appropriate energetic guide – slightly "above" us, but not too elevated as to be beyond our reach and comprehension – to encourage and steer us at each stage of our ascension back to Source.

We might assume that our spiritual self is always perfectly

happy and contented, not having a care in the world. I do not have a firm grasp of the metaphysics here, but I can testify from profound personal experiences in which I was shown (and, more to the point, felt) an element of my soul's perspective that even aspects of our spirit – perhaps those closest to us in vibration – may benefit from healing. If, for example, you have endured lifetime after lifetime of distressing events, your soul may in some way be affected by your misery.

Similarly, discordant resonances of the division of spirit and matter may be carried in your physical body as well as, perhaps, in a small portion of your discarnate self. And then, if they are not on the earth plane, there is the matter of your twin flame – your divine partner, the other half of your individualized God presence from whom you separated to undergo your own testing experiences. They may have met with equally challenging lifetimes and, while they may have achieved considerable balance and harmony to enable them now to reside in the ascended realms, some degree of healing might still be helpful to both of you.

You may not understand from your current viewpoint what sort of soul healing needs to be carried out and how, and nor do you need to delve into "monads", "soul groups" and so on. Simply trust that this next ceremony will cover every currently relevant eventuality. You might request understanding during your quiet time afterwards. Listen to messages from your heart: as you strive towards unconditional acceptance and love of yourself, you may be given rewarding insights.

You might also experience communication between different levels of yourself, which can be quite fascinating, in order to achieve resolution and peace. For instance, you may have agreed prior to your incarnation to take on a very demanding role. Part of your being may be blissfully happy with what you are doing and content for you to continue serving in this way. Another part, however, perhaps in an even higher dimension and having a more expansive perspective, might be acutely aware of the need for your increasingly onerous task to come to an end. All of you must be accepting of whatever decision you know at your Light center is the absolute best for you right now.

I AM my multi-dimensional self. Through Divine Light and Grace and in the name of the Creator, I ask for help in sending healing (*or* I send healing) to myself in all lifetimes, including this one, and in all time frames, realities, dimensions and levels of consciousness. (x3)

I acknowledge those aspects of me which have remained unresolved and in pain or suffering as a result of a lack of my love, compassion and understanding, and which are exerting an influence on my multi-dimensional self today. I now accept and infuse them with Love to bring healing and joyful integration. (x3)

My being is pulsating with Light. I AM whole. I AM Love, harmony and peace. Bliss emanates from every facet of my being, from every aspect of my divine and physical self. I AM spirit and matter. (x3)

I AM Light and Love. May the Source of healing fill me with unconditional love to touch the hearts of others and so bring them nearer to God. (x3)

So be it. So it is done. So it is.

Chapter 5

Forgiveness

When we are in the flowing stream of unconditional love, forgiveness never has to enter the equation because pure love is beyond criticism of ourselves or others. It accepts from its heart all beings in their unique expression of divinity, and does not form grudges, malice or deep-seated resentments.

How many of us can honestly say we always exist in that state of grace each day? Even though we may be pretty balanced and centered much of the time now, what about the past? Most of us have carried the odd bag of niggles at some stage. We may even be lugging heavy suitcase loads around from previous lives without knowing it. And as human beings we do not necessarily always find it easy to respond compassionately straight away to extreme provocation.

People who go through great adversity which tests their patient, loving nature may find themselves uncharacteristically fighting to assert their forgiving side. It can be very hard reaching a place of peace. Resolution may come in stages as others' viewpoints and beliefs are acknowledged and it is accepted that everyone has been and is doing the best they can, even if their actions make that seem on occasion impossible to comprehend.

Forgiveness is often about reminding ourselves that we usually respond to what we consider unjust because we are looking at an incomplete picture. Small irritations, such as a partner's noisy cough during a heavy cold, can soon get out of hand if we are in rosy health and have forgotten how draining a hacking cough can be.

The woman at the supermarket checkout may be creating a

drama over her shopping and making you annoyingly late for an appointment because she has received bad news. And the person who attacks you for being at the center of their woes is not waging war against you but is choosing to ignore the real cause of their frustration: themselves – although they might also be holding a mirror up for you to look hard at your own attitudes.

You will probably never in this lifetime be able to paint in every blank spot on the canvas. Simply know that your soul will have chosen a wide range of exacting scenarios for you to help you grow your angel wings.

Until we can flutter our wings as gracefully as swans do, we may discover that some emotional hangovers from major trauma in this lifetime take a little while to let go. Minor irritations, on the other hand, for which we have no deep-seated attachments, can be transformed surprisingly quickly if we have the courage to face them square on and the determination to stay with the healing process should it become a little uncomfortable. This next technique is another variation on the feeling theme.

Retire to your quiet, favorite place where you will not be disturbed for a while, and sit or lie down. Set your intent to open your heart to forgiveness. Invoke the violet flame and then bring to mind the circumstances surrounding your stress – the people, place and situation – and begin to feel into the emotion they trigger.

Feel, feel, feel it to the core and avoid turning away from it, whether through fear, because you think it is unspiritual or you are not keen on the churning sensation in your stomach. Even when you are wobbly – it can be like navigating through monstrously large ocean waves – continue concentrating. Maintain this focus and eventually the emotion will lose its power, diminish and ultimately fade away to nothing.

When this starts to happen, you might re-emphasize your wish to release old emotions that have been pulling you down, by stating "I forgive you/myself." Feel the forgiveness in your being as deeply as you did the original emotion. When its high vibrational energy has transformed and healed, you will then reach a point of equilibrium at which you no longer experience either feeling. At this stage you can hold everyone involved within your heart with love.

By the end of a session you may be amazed at how replaying those scenes in your head which used to cause you so much annoyance no longer elicit any response. It can be a liberating moment. If other emotions surface – sometimes a dominant emotion can mask other less obtrusive ones – these can be dealt with in the same manner, like the proverbial peeling away of onion layers.

Forgiveness of all

Forgiveness plays such an important part in our ability to interact joyfully with the world. While we might have let go of bitterness towards other people and we now feel at peace with ourselves, we nevertheless might also consider what impact our less than ideal behavior, either intentional or unintentional, may have had in the past on those with whom we have come into contact. Even a casual remark, which we might assume would have been brushed off like a speck of dust from a collar, could to a sensitive person have felt like a knife jab.

A broader awareness of the energetic ramifications of forgiveness (giving and receiving it) is an extremely high vibrational power tool to carry in your spiritual kit. Having the capacity to transform hearts and minds, and set souls glowing with pleasure, is an awesome human skill. Continually forgiving everyone each and every day, including yourself (none of us is perfect and never will be this time around), is obviously a great policy to adopt. But as well as that, you can achieve a huge amount more by broadcasting your forgiveness on a universal scale across time.

The following ceremony provides you with the opportunity

to heal distress and rifts caused during your current and previous lives, although at a personality level you may not be aware of most of them. It does not matter: what is most important is your acceptance that you've slipped up now and then, together with your willingness to make amends. This once-for-all cleansing will probably rule out the need for further in-depth work on forgiveness, assuming you have already dealt with large-scale conflicts. Say it with real conviction and add specific details if you wish to acknowledge some individual(s) in particular. You might also like to include future lives in your wording.

Through my divine self, under the Law of Grace and in the Name of God/Goddess of Love and Light, I command that:

my negative, low vibrational, unenlightened thoughts, words, deeds and emotions and their impact on me and on others in all lifetimes, including this one, and in all time frames and realities, that lead, will lead or have led to my and others' imbalance and dis-ease, and which no longer serve our highest good, be transmuted by the power of the Violet Flame and Violet Fire into Light and Love NOW. May healing take place, bringing optimum health and wellbeing. (x3)

Through my I AM Presence I ask forgiveness of those I have ever consciously or unconsciously, deliberately or inadvertently, hurt in any way. And I forgive those who have hurt me or whom I have allowed to hurt me. (x3)

I forgive myself and everyone everything always. (x3)

May the past, present and future, the NOW, be pure and filled with unconditional Love and Light. (x3)

I AM Love and Light. (x3)

Should you have extensive ongoing difficulties, you could create an alternative ceremony in which you solicit help in allowing forgiveness into your heart as well as sending it to those who are presenting you with challenges.

You might also invoke the violet flame for each of them, requesting that it continue burning until you have resolved your differences. After that the ideal is to face one another for a frank discussion, but if this is not feasible you could write a letter explaining how you feel.

If the person you need to address has passed over, you can still compose a letter. Imagine them picking it up and reading it – and read it they will!

As in the Mahatma attunement in the last chapter, it is a case of accepting everything you have done, and understanding that you are the sensational person you are today because of each choice you have ever made. It is no good disowning actions you are not particularly proud of or sweeping them under the carpet. Your soul will want you to account for them at some stage, so perhaps better now than later.

This reminds me of a period Louise and I went through in which we felt compelled to apologize for our behavior many, many years previously – in fact it was so long ago that most of our friends and family looked at us in disbelief, wondering what had come over us. My step-brother found it quite hilarious that I should say sorry for consistently beating him at various games when we were youngsters, but deep inside I knew that I had not always treated him with the respect he deserved. I could so easily have encouraged him instead of allowing my competitive streak always to dominate our play together.

It was important to me that I should admit my mistakes and mend the energetic fractures. And the reason? It is generally agreed that on passing over from the earth plane an individual goes through a review during which they assess without criticism what has transpired during their life in the physical dimension. According to the spiritual law of cause and effect, it must then be decided how any accrued karma is worked out during the next incarnation.

Spiritual seekers who are keen to leap off the karmic wheel

and continue on their evolutionary journey in other dimensions (although they may still choose to return to earth as part of their service to the Creator) really need to settle their karmic debts this time around and not carry any over.

In order to help the process along they may experience periodic life reviews while still in their current incarnation, which come in the form of opportunities to cancel out negative karma and increase their measures of good. Once you are aware of this, you will soon recognize the additional importance of family gatherings – they are excellent occasions for clocking up brownie points!

These periodic reviews can also feel like grieving times, a sort of death while still alive because you have successfully completed a series of tasks required of you and, rather than waiting until the end of your current incarnation, you are now releasing what you no longer need to carry you forwards. If it has been with you for a long time, you may feel an initial pang at its loss.

Forgiveness in our world is naturally crucial, but equally important is showing gratitude, especially to people you may have taken for granted or not thanked adequately. Seize each chance you get to fill those who have played their roles in your life drama so well with oceans of love. It can be as easy as "Thank you for all you have done for me..."

If someone remains unwilling to let bygones be bygones, visualize them surrounded by a pink cloud and leave them be. You have done your best; it is now up to them to deal with anxieties of their own making.

For anyone you are no longer in touch with, a quiet thought recognizing their generosity, is always worth doing too. The love impulse will undoubtedly reach them.

You could also create a special ceremony in which you send love and thanks to those, known and/or unknown, who have walked through life with you. Or maybe a ceremony concentrating on joy would be a nice idea. A celebration of delight and happiness will attract even more blessings to you.

Daily dusting off

As a form of ongoing Light support, you might consider finishing each day by casting your mind back over what you have done and whom you have met. Were you governed by your heart at all times or did your mouth run away with you? You might feel a twinge of embarrassment at some of your escapades or slightly aggrieved at someone else's.

Whatever has transpired, bless your experiences and be grateful for what you have gained from them. Forgiveness may seem too grand a word to describe how you process them here, but there is an aspect of it which is part of accepting your day's high and low points and moving on.

You can also dust yourself off by calling in the violet flame. It is comparable to taking your litter home after a picnic and disposing of it responsibly. This invocation, which I picked up many years ago from a source I unfortunately can no longer remember, serves this purpose very well:

Through All that I AM, I invoke the Violet Flame to transmute, balance and harmonize the discordant or low vibrational energy I have projected, released and taken on board since last night/this morning and transmute it into Light.

You could then follow on with:

I AM the Violet Flame and Fire of Light now and throughout tonight.

If you can go into your heart center and remain for a while in that place of stillness after invoking the violet flame for yourself,

Mother Earth and her inhabitants (imagine the world enveloped in violet), your body will relax and allow the high vibrational energy to do whatever purification is necessary. That can be a lovely way to drift off to sleep.

Chapter 6

What is ego?

How do you view "ego"? Do you think it drags you down? Do you honor it for the myriad insights it throws up every single day? Have you considered what it might actually be?

Ego is often associated with people who talk at length about themselves and who are interested solely in ensuring their own welfare, maybe at the expense of others – although it is likely they are really crying out for affection because, if they could but admit it to themselves, they have very low self-esteem. In this sort of context ego equates with an overinflated view of self or a domineering personality fully immersed in a lower dimensional life.

For those treading an overtly spiritual path ego may be thought of slightly differently, perhaps as the shadow or dark side to the Light self. Some regard it at best as a pest and at worst a fiend to wrestle and fight constantly, an entity to get rid of at all costs and ultimately to destroy – like St George fighting the dragon. It can be hugely exasperating when ego and so-called "negative" ego seem persistently to motivate envy, pride, self-deprecation and so on.

But is it genuinely a destructive element which continually sabotages spirituality? If you prefer to give everything in the universe a positive spin, turn this concept on its head and you end up with something akin to a best friend who has known you a very long time and who will unerringly direct you with pinpoint accuracy again and again to where healing is required.

Your ego can be seen as an inner torch which illuminates your healing path by highlighting every restriction you need to free yourself from. It can be construed as one of the best guides you will ever have in this dimension, and how you interpret its communications may determine how quickly you move on to the next stage of learning.

My own view of ego was always of the conventional "what a nuisance" type until a spanner was thrown in the works one day. I had nothing of concern on my mind, and yet emotionally charged feelings of self-importance kept annoying me. Sensing they must have been provoked for a reason and should not be dismissed, I went into Word Power mode and stated, "I'm better than everyone else!" Straight away my mood changed and I was plunged into distressing feelings of desolation.

These were accompanied by an image of myself, small and alone, in a bleak, black void aeons ago. All I could hear from the distant figure in that place of isolation was the lament, "I'm so lonely." The scene was then transformed into an internal, rock-solid knowingness about what the picture represented.

The explanation went along these lines. At some point in our descension from Source, our masculine and feminine energies were separated from one another, each of the resulting "twin flames" then going on to experience the gamut of lower density life away from the other. In order to compensate for the potentially colossal sense of loss at being parted, an "ego" was joined to each to help them feel complete again.

Not only did this ego act as a substitute for the other twin flame, it also served as a form of protection in a very different environment: it enabled the incarnated soul to adapt to coping with physicality. And, since the divine intention was for us to perceive Mother/Father God in every atom of Creation, it gave us a wealth of opportunities to understand thoroughly the nature of unconditional love.

Somewhere along the line, balance was lost as individuals found themselves captivated by the lure of the body's senses. Ego then had to raise its voice to be heard. The emotions we associate with Light-less behavior were its way of alerting us to take stock and prevent us from careering too far off course. And its message remains the same today: if we listen to its promptings, we can find the origins of our disharmony and therefore a means of regaining equilibrium.

For anyone interested in spiritual evolution, an important prerequisite to functioning in the fifth dimension and above is that twin flames should once again unite. However a full, blissful union can only happen once ego is off the scene. Before then, only partial mergers can be achieved.

With such a tantalizing prospect in sight, you would imagine it would be plain sailing for us to cope without our ego, but it has been with us as a caring partner for so long that we naturally have great affection for and attraction to one another.

For this reason a number of people are reluctant to release it completely, perhaps at some level fearing the pain of another separation. Grief can certainly surface when you begin to view ego with compassion as friend not foe, but this quickly subsides when the connection with your higher self is strengthened. If you are one of those people who believe this is your last incarnation on earth, you may also experience a certain amount of sadness at relinquishing ego because it marks the end of a grand adventure as a third-dimensional human.

I am not altogether sure how ego can best be described. You might imagine it as another subtle body or as an energetic bolt-on forming an integral part of your physical expression. Perhaps the easiest way to explain it is to use a metaphor, that of an ancient computer program.

The more we demonstrate our mastery and upgrade ourselves with modern, higher level programs through our self-development, the more outdated the ego program will become until eventually it will be obsolete. At that point its role as mediator between the lower self and higher self will be redundant, because the two selves will be intimately linked and in many cases, like the twin flames, will also be merging (more of that shortly).

Having been introduced to this new interpretation of ego, my immediate reaction was to conduct a ceremony in which I asked for mine to be lovingly unbolted and taken away in one fell swoop. It was perhaps a naive request but, having said that, for the next two days I felt entirely at peace with myself.

Whilst the serenity did not last, it did give me confirmation that the ceremony had not been a totally silly idea. I therefore revised the wording and arrived at a version which strives to cater for the means by which ego may have been manifested. Ego will ultimately be transmuted when we have let go of fear and can love unconditionally.

It is obviously a very personal slant on a process which is really about expanding your consciousness, but the aim of the ceremony is to help your enlightenment along. If we relinquished our ego all at once and were not adequately prepared, we might not cope with the intensity of Light we would be exposed to. And yet if we can surrender constantly to the love and wisdom of our divine self, the stages of releasing our ego can certainly be eased and, in time, dispensed with altogether. The choice is ours.

However you view ego, I hope you are encouraged to be gentle on that facet of you which knows how much polishing of yourself there is still to do.

Dearest Creator: I thank you for the experience of duality, of living on Earth. I thank you for your blessings and gifts. (x3)

Through All that I AM, I call upon Archangel Metatron and the ascended realms of Love and Light who are supporting humankind in raising our vibrations and consciousness. I also call upon angels and archangels of healing, my healing guides and mentors, my monad, soul and guardian angel… I ask for your help in transmuting ego through Love and transforming it into Light. (x3)

Through Divine Light and Grace, and in the Name of

God/Goddess, I release, with love, ego from my core, from my body, cells, cell memories, DNA, subtle bodies and other parts of my being where it no longer serves my highest good. I release all energetic residues, imprinting, coding, thoughts, thinking patterns, behaviors, emotions, feelings, desires and ways of manifesting connected with and/or directed by ego which are no longer appropriate for me. (x3)

I thank my ego for its help and sustenance, but now through my divine godself I invoke the Violet Flame to transmute it and transform it into Light quickly and easily according to whatever is most suitable for my highest spiritual interests and evolution. (x3)

I now nourish myself with my divine Light and the Healing Energy of Source. I see perfection and Love in every facet of creation, including myself. I open to the infinite wisdom of the universe. (x3)

I AM unconditional love. Thank you dearest Mother/Father of One and All. (x3)

Less I, more we

On some occasions, when our spiritual connection is strong, our higher self may seem very close while at other times it might as well be in another cosmos for all we can discern. This is due to the natural rhythms of the universe: after an active period of learning a quieter phase often ensues to allow us space in which to absorb properly what we have taken on board. During these integration periods we may feel as though we are going backwards spiritually speaking and it can be confusing, especially when we are eager to recapture the excitement of moving onwards.

A sense of distance from our higher self can also be due to our ego's less than subtle messages pressing us to delve even further into our inner resources. Frustration and feeling cut off from everyone and everything are often signs to dig deeper. In cases like this, although it may not seem like it, an ego may in fact be trying to deconstruct barriers rather than to erect them. It is probably pointing out another layer of lower density energy to be pared away. "Lower density energy" is obviously subjective: you are continually evolving and moving up the spiral of consciousness, so what might at one stage have been "higher density energy" may at a later date become incompatible with your lighter energetic make-up and need to be discarded.

As you increase your rate of vibration and gradually function at higher and higher frequencies, you will sometimes make a marked shift to a new position. Here you may experience a sort of radio interference or universe static because you have not yet learned to tune yourself in properly from this more "elevated" position to your higher self. This too can cause you momentarily to feel as though you have lost your way.

The trick is to carry on clearing the airwaves by continually transmuting or letting go of energy that is no longer benefiting you. We might be very pleased with ourselves for having made astounding progress, but we can never sit on our laurels for long because each learning stage always brings a fresh set of circumstances for us to demonstrate our skills and acquire new ones.

There is an additional benefit to making yourself as clear and high vibrational a vessel as you can. Expansion of your consciousness, or accessing more of your divine wisdom, assists you in creating the heaven on earth so many people talk about these days without you having to wait years to accomplish it.

What this actually means is that you can invite more and more of your spiritual essence into your physical form *now* and begin combining the two to fulfill your enormous potential in the earthly dimension. The less ego you have, the easier it is for this to happen.

I was extremely doubtful about such an extraordinary possibility. Spiritual phenomena described in books can seem so hypothetical, unreal and irrelevant, but every now and then you can be presented with overwhelming personal evidence which swiftly converts abstract theory into belief. The following experiences helped do just that for me.

The first happened at night. I was sleeping lightly. Then, what can only be described as two massive bolts of electricity shot right through me from head to foot. The shock and surprise, never mind the sheer force of the energy, catapulted my body into the air. A few seconds later it seemed as though a switch was pulled and I was hooked up to what felt like the spiritual equivalent of the national power grid. There were no subtleties here. It was a magnificent demonstration, if ever I needed one, of the power of Spirit – or perhaps I should say Spirit and Matter meeting and combining.

The second experience happened over a period of time and was a little more restrained. It began with a lucid dream heralded by a circle of pure blue sky. In the dream I was aware of being very low down on the ground, at a level with the hem of an exquisite sky blue robe. As my gaze rose upwards, so the dress continued to materialize until I reached a face whose stunning features caused me to linger over them. For some reason I had been anticipating a man's physiognomy, but instead I was met by that of a serenely beautiful woman. I knew this was an important image I should remember.

Many months later I was tossing and turning during the night before a workshop in which I was due to speak. I was aware of presences in the room, and found it difficult to sleep. At one point my consciousness looked upwards to a place beyond the stars, far out in the heavens. A bright blue circle came into view and beamed down information and energy, at which moment I had to laugh because I was going to have to survive the next day on very little rest.

When the time came for me to present my material at the workshop I felt an influx of spiritual energy. It was particularly noticeable because I could not switch off my internal healing mechanism and electric currents fired off left, right and center.

I ignored them as best I could, stood up and proceeded to give my talk without nerves or hesitation, which was quite remarkable given the extent of my anxiety beforehand – I had not done any public speaking for a long time. As soon as I sat down again, the energy departed and I was back with my more familiar self.

Three months later the bright blue circle showed up once again during the night, though on this occasion I sensed it was much closer than previously – no longer zillions of light years away, but more like on the roof of the house.

Fast forward a few weeks to a gathering at a friend's. We decided to have a meditation and at the outset I affirmed to myself in a quite relaxed fashion something along the lines of: "Over to you, my Higher Self," and left it at that, fully expecting the next hour would be spent enjoying quiet contemplation.

All was going to plan until the very end of the meditation when the lady in the sky blue dress turned up – there was no mistaking her – and sat right in front of me. Such waves of love emanated from her that I could not help but respond in like manner. In the scenario played out in my mind, she took my right hand and held it tenderly for a few minutes.

Next she grasped my left hand and in that instant I heard what sounded like a hatch shutter being drawn back quickly just outside my field of vision. And then I was hurtling forwards through space, and my heart started to beat frighteningly hard and fast, so much so that for a brief second I wondered whether I was going to have a seizure. Recognizing that this strange experience was really nothing to fear, I breathed energy through my body down to my feet and into Mother Earth.

On returning home I observed with delight a small circle of spiritual energy the color of a penetratingly sky blue by my left side (traditionally considered the "receiving" side). It was as brilliant, solid and real as any phenomenon I have witnessed on the physical plane, and marked the last, confirmatory phase in an amazing sequence of events.

My interpretation goes something like this. In spiritual terms the color sky blue is associated with the soul. In the dream a connection was made with an aspect of that divine spark which was presented as the figure of the radiant woman. I was at her feet, not standing up in front of her, suggesting that energetically we were not yet on the same vibration, or at least the vibration required for a permanent merger could not be maintained. This was why the workshop assistance was only temporary – I was not yet able to hold the higher frequencies.

Gradually, over the succeeding months my vibration must have been raised, which explains why the blue circles at night appeared to travel towards me. The process must have continued until spirit and matter resonated sufficiently closely to one another for a successful and permanent merger during the meditation (after which life certainly went up a notch or two).

Some people refer to these types of merging experience as "initiations", but you do not have to undergo them in such a physical or dramatic manner for them to occur. The faster your vibration, the closer it will match that of your higher self and therefore any energy blends will be very comfortable and may be imperceptible. A sudden, unexpected decision to take up a new hobby or branch out boldly in your life may well be the result of such an event. Or you may simply feel more at peace with who you are.

If you are ready to start opening up to your higher self, a useful invocation to say each day is:

"I AM my Higher Self," or
"I open to my Higher Self."

This may, should you need it, help you feel more at ease with the idea of inviting your spiritual essence closer to you.

At this stage it is also important to acknowledge Mother Earth regularly. It is all very well thinking about what is going on "up" there among the celestial spheres, so to speak, and getting caught up in the excitement of spiritual energies, but unless we are fully grounded on our lovely planet in the here and now we may not be ready for a merger of any sort.

Part of our education is to master living with one foot firmly in the physical camp and one foot firmly in the metaphysical camp. Self-assurance is required so that ultimately and paradoxically we can become all spirit and all matter simultaneously. Our higher self understands this well, so another affirmation might be:

"I surrender to my Higher Self,"

which means you are trusting it to take greater control of the rudder. That should make life more tranquil for you, as long as you do not keep trying to snatch it back every time you have a wobble.

To take the theme on a stage further you might devise a ceremony in which you express your love for your higher self. A starting phrase which came to mind was:

"From my heart to my soul and from my soul to my heart, I AM Spirit and Matter…"

As this particular ceremony could potentially be the most intimate in this book, I leave it to you to follow on with your own words – or perhaps choose your favourite poems, songs, etc to help convey your renewed commitment to your godself.

Chapter 7

Creating from the heart

As your ego becomes less intrusive and you increasingly surrender to your higher self, you will experience much greater inner and outer harmony than you did in your early spiritual schooling. You will enjoy longer periods of stability and a reduced susceptibility to swing wildly with the natural rhythms of the universe's energetic cycles.

For those occasions when you find yourself teetering on the brink of going off course again, listen to your body and emotions: they may have a helpful message for you, such as take life less seriously or make it more playful.

After that a good technique to bring yourself back into balance is to place both hands on your heart center. Ground yourself, feel love in your heart for who you are, and then affirm with conviction:

"I AM my Higher Self. I honor myself and I love myself unconditionally."

Allow your lower self once again to be enfolded by your higher divine self, and hold this position until you feel a gentle warmth all over.

Concentrating in this way, albeit very briefly, on your lower and higher minds resonating in concord can shift energetic blocks and get you back on an even keel. Eventually they will be as one – releasing ego, bringing in your spiritual essence, and reuniting with your twin flame are part of the same ongoing process. Until you have cleared every necessary obstacle for it to reach its natural conclusion, partial mergers will be the order of the day and you will probably need to recalibrate yourself periodically.

Harnessing the combined power of your higher and lower self via your heart center is also the key to creating every beauteous thing you desire for yourself – it can be done only with and through love. The ceremonies, attunements and decrees already outlined in this book can be part of this creativity, and with a little extra thought they can be usefully mixed and matched.

To give you an example here is a four-stage approach to manifesting the best, including abundance, for yourself. If you can manage it, you can go for the lot in one session, but it might be easier at first if you left a few days in between stages. It might seem cumbersome now, but in time you will be able to condense the complete process into a few minutes or even seconds. Once you have done the third part, it can probably be omitted in future.

(a) Clear blockages

If you have underlying problems with your self-worth, they may undermine your plans. So test the water by saying to yourself, ideally in Word Power mode:

"I am worthy of abundance."

If there is no reaction, press a little harder with:

"I am worthy of x" ("x" being whatever it is you wish to receive or achieve).

Or, as mentioned in Chapter 3, state the opposite of what you intend for yourself.

Play around with these phrases until you have satisfied yourself there is nothing more to be done at the moment. Be honest, and try not to be in too much of a rush to move on to the next stages. Time spent now on uncovering hang-ups will pay dividends in the long run.

It's rather like decorating a house. The boring sanding down, filling in of cracks, priming etc has to be executed properly first before the glamorous outer coat painting, otherwise the end result will look botched, unprofessional and disappointing, and will not last.

(b) Cut ties and acknowledge your path

Do you feel you may still have ties with a vow of poverty taken in a past life? Given the large number of religions there have been throughout the history of humankind it is not surprising that energetic residues of ancient vows of privation are still reverberating around the world today. Such pledges usually translate into general poverty consciousness in this life: people are uncomfortable with any form of plenty and not just with large amounts of money.

You can ask Archangel Michael to sever remaining cords and give you healing. Or, once you have read this book through, you might revisit Chapters 1 and 8 and, if you have not already done so, use the decrees as appropriate.

At the same time acknowledge with compassion the you who agreed to such restrictive measures on your freedom (you probably did it with the best of intentions at the time) and express gratitude for the breadth of learning you have derived from the experience. And if need be bring in Word Power to uncover other reasons for the choices you currently make that are impacting on what you materialize for yourself.

(c) Conduct a ceremony

When I first mooted a co-creation ceremony, I thought maybe something similar to a healing attunement would be suitable. My reasoning was that perhaps co-creation channels could be brought on-line in the same way as healing ones.

When I came to the wording I was guided to take the idea a little further and to describe a matrix, or web of light, between the higher and lower self which would act as a vehicle for bringing thought into physical manifestation. This phenomenon is something I recall having seen around the face of a friend several years ago. At the time I did not know what it was: in fact I was totally perplexed because the shimmering golden mesh seemed to be around the outside of her head and extend inwards, into her skin.

Later guidance, which gave me much deeper understanding and forms the backbone of this section, was followed up by a bit of research. This seemed to confirm that other people have also picked up on our connection to an interdimensional web which some have called the "cosmic lattice".

Peggy Phoenix Dubro in Chapter 3 of *Elegant Empowerment: Evolution of Consciousness*, explains it as "the unlimited universal energy source" and suggests that each of us has a personal connection via our own "Universal Calibration Lattice®" which "permeates our very existence, right down to the cellular level, and beyond, into our subatomic field" (see Books and websites for details if you are interested in reading further about this topic).

This is potentially a complex subject, but suffice to say here that the cosmic lattice allows us to tap into boundless energy and therefore into infinite creative potential.

The next ceremony focuses very simply on recognizing the existence of the co-creative lattice to which you, your higher self and other beings in different dimensions are all linked. Once the concept has filtered through to your waking consciousness and you feel at ease with it, your belief and focus will automatically bolster your connections.

This in turn will make it easier for you to access the lattice and you can then enjoy the benefits which that will automatically bring. For those who understand the system, a working knowledge of how the lattice functions can bring about amazingly quick manifestation.

Positive thinking and affirmations often associated with co-creation and other spiritual observances, as well as feeling good about yourself, are not just about you getting your heart, mind and emotions in order. They are actual impulses of energy or messages sent along the lattice's lines and intersections.

They are received and acted upon by other consciousnesses and beings connected to you via what is like a cosmic internet. An added bonus to you raising your vibrations is that your higher frequencies will be transmitted universally, meaning you can affect people on the other side of the world, urging them onwards in their own spiritual development.

Similarly, doubts and fears, even dithering about what to do, will also send out signals to be picked up. If these are of a similar strength to the positive messages, they may cancel the positive ones out – or at least cause your entire project to be put on hold until it becomes clear exactly which route you wish to pursue. (Under the divine law of free will no one, apart from you, can decide your course of action.)

If they are stronger, and fear can be pretty forceful, then the universe will assume those instructions are your preferred intentions and will act accordingly, probably bringing you what you least intended but which you feared the most. This is why it is so important to clarify, as far as possible, within yourself what it is you are seeking, to be precise in what you ask for and to maintain your vision.

The best policy is to send everything via your higher self, because it will transmit perfect, robust signals for what is in your very best interests. If you can keep the channels clear between you, there won't be any crossed wires to cause interference.

Here is the the co-creation attunement:

Dear Mother/Father God, Lord of Creation, I call upon you

through the entirety of my being to establish a link with my co-creative Higher Self for the highest good of all. (x3)

Through my Higher Self I invoke Archangel Metatron to oversee the process and I invite angels of Love and Light, elementals of Love and Light, and other cosmic beings of the highest vibration appropriate for me in this very moment to assist us. (x3)

We invoke the Violet Flame to transmute energy in and around us and transform it into Light. (x3)

I now reach to my Higher Self and my Higher Self reaches to me. I now touch my Higher Self and my Higher Self touches me. We are one and we forge and illuminate a co-creative matrix by and through which we create from our heart center in every void, dimension, reality and time frame for the benefit of all beings. (x3)

This matrix is now sealed and blessed by Archangel Metatron. (x3)

This matrix is now strengthened and confirmed in our being. (x3)

Thanks to Mother/Father God, the Fount of Creation, Archangel Metatron, angels, elementals and other beings of Love and Light. (x3)

So be it. So it is done. So it is.

Louise's experience of this ceremony was that it immediately evoked powerful emotions. She spent the next few hours trying desperately hard to mark school examination papers but all the while undergoing waves of downloads and masses of energetic clearing, presumably in order to bring fully on line large sections of her lattice.

(d) Visualize and verbalize
The last stage is to think about your co-creation project and to employ your senses to make it as tangible as you can and to really

boost your message to the universe. Can you touch it, feel it, smell and see, even taste, it in your mind?

Once you have sketched this blue print, transfer it to your heart center where it can be reassessed for motive. Ensure that what you are wishing to manifest joyfully is still in alignment with your higher self. You might also assign it a special symbol or picture that you can visualize again at a later date.

An excellent method of covering off these last-minute checks is to imagine your higher self standing in front of you and holding your hands. Look deep into the eyes of this Love which is your truth and knows you far better than anyone else possibly can, and say, with meaning, "I am worthy of x" ("x" being your objective).

If you can hold the gaze of your higher self without needing to look away out of embarrassment or lack of belief in yourself, and without wriggling inside or feeling uncomfortable, then you have done your preparation.

Next, release your image from your heart center and imagine it being transferred to the cosmic lattice, perhaps in a dazzling burst of energy or amid a volley of noisy fireworks. Affirm your intention once more:

We now invoke God's co-creative energy to create 'x' from our heart center for our highest good and the highest good of all. Thanks be to God and every being of creation for assisting and transforming.

After that, let it go and allow the cosmos to provide for you. The part of us that needs to be busy doing can find this the hardest task to perform. If impatience or doubts creep in, renew and strengthen your intent by visualizing your symbol and surrounding it by Light. Then, again, let it go and do not be tempted to cling on to it otherwise you will put out conflicting messages via the lattice. Were you to be asked to undertake an important job and you agreed, you would expect to get on with it without being pestered every minute of the day, wouldn't you? If you kept being harassed, you might even feel inclined to delay matters.

This Light technique came in handy when Tom and Liz were wrestling with the effects of "car cloning". A vehicle – probably stolen – of the same make, model and color as theirs and with the same registration plate was being driven in and around London by someone who had scant respect for legal parking restrictions. As a consequence parking tickets regularly winged their way to their house, invariably to Liz as their car was registered in her name.

She spent an inordinate amount of time writing letters and making phone calls, explaining to car park owners and police officers that she lived far away from where the parking offences were being committed, and more often than not she could provide concrete alibis. Everyone she spoke to was very sympathetic and she never had to pay any fines, but it soon became evident that car cloning is such a commonplace problem that little seems to be done to catch the perpetrators. And so the tickets kept coming.

This was not good enough for Liz. She was fed up having to account for herself whenever another official brown envelope plopped through the letter box. And she certainly did not see why someone out there should shirk personal responsibility and knowingly pass the buck to a stranger. She did not blame this individual or feel any animosity towards them. She merely wished that their behavior should stop.

As they lived 200 miles from London, all she could do was mentally surround her image of the London car in Light and ask for a resolution to their problem that would be in the highest interests of everyone concerned. Each time she thought about it she repeated these simple steps, trusting implicitly in a peaceful, undramatic outcome at whatever moment was convenient to the universe.

Several weeks went by and then one evening the phone rang and Tom answered it. A London policeman was asking him where their car was parked. Tom of course replied that it was in the driveway adjacent to their house, to which the officer let out a triumphant snort of glee.

Apparently a patrol had spotted a car with a defective headlight. Although having a headlight that does not work properly is technically an offence and potentially it can be hazardous when driving in the dark, it is not the most heinous of crimes.

On this particular occasion the police decided not to pass it by and spoke to the driver. As a matter of routine they ran a quick check which showed the car's owner to live far away. This seemed rather suspicious to them, so they then conducted a little more research and soon came across files of Liz's reports. Bingo! The clone culprit was caught red-handed.

I wonder what the odds were of these precise set of circum-stances, which were so favorable for Tom and Liz, to present themselves at just the right time? And I cannot help smiling at the irony of a headlight being at the center of the affair.

Chapter 8

The joy of crystals

The inspiration for this chapter came from the following unusual experience.

A slender young woman, wearing a delicate, flowing garment in pastel greens and yellows and cut into a series of jagged shapes at the bottom, escorted me into a cavern brimming with crystals of spectacular shapes, sizes and colors. Her graceful feminine energy, which seemed to emanate from her dress as well as from her person, was as captivating as jewelled cobwebs caught in the early morning sun.

In the next instant, back out under a midnight sky, I gazed up towards the stars and was aware of the cave crystals sending out information about earth and receiving intelligence from the universe. Tears rolled down my cheeks as an inner knowingness told me that I had once been united with spiritual beings of the mineral kingdom, perhaps when I myself had been one of their number.

And then, in this strange moment of recognition, I felt a precious link with a spiritual body I sensed I had already created in the crystal realm and from which I was now receiving knowledge of my existence there.

I opened my eyes and looked in awe at the large piece of quartz I had been holding. Its serene presence continued to envelop me as I sat for a little while longer in silence, contemplating my vision. It had been quite a response to an innocuous question about the crystal's nature and how we might co-operate together...

Light bodies' attunement

Crystals, as anyone who uses them regularly will know, are keen to interact with us, for they have an important calling: they too are expanding their consciousness, by helping creatures on the planet as well as Mother Earth herself. Acting rather like radio transponders, they relay messages from many dimensions and convey them in a form we find easy to cope with on the physical plane.

Taking this idea of interdimensional collaboration a stage further, can you envisage linking empathically with every dimension and therefore, by implication, with each level of your divine self? It is not as absurd a question to ask as it may at first sound. Here is some food for thought. It is a very basic interpretation (I am only skimming the surface for details) of a spiritual phenomenon that may explain how it may be possible.

Imagine that at each stage of your journey from Source in the outbreath of God, you created what may be called a "Light vessel" or "Light body" for yourself. Once you fulfilled your role at one level, you carefully preserved your unique insights and some of your essence before moving on to the next. (You may not necessarily have traveled from the highest dimension in single steps "down", but may have jumped around, perhaps from the twelfth to the fifth to the first to the sixth, and so on.)

In this context the Light body can be viewed as a transcendent spiritual receptacle housing the accumulated wealth of personal learning, positive karma where appropriate, wisdom and experience – a being's creative potential fully expressed – that an individuated spark of Source amasses while in a particular realm. As a vessel of Light, it vibrates at the highest possible frequency consonant with the dimension in which it exists. (I wonder whether the current phenomenon of "orbs" is somehow connected here.)

Now consider reconnecting yourself to those Light bodies you have acquired during your spiritual evolution. You would be like an archaeologist thousands of years in the future finding and, even more incredibly, decoding ancient computer data files that contained long lost treasure troves of information about life centuries ago.

If you think back to the multi-dimensional cosmic lattice, your Light bodies can be viewed as portions of the web that are joined together through intersections on different planes. Or you might simply visualize them as multicolored spheres linked together by a mesh of golden threads.

Focusing on them during an attunement causes communication channels to be opened up and reinforced. Ultimately your Light bodies may be brought into alignment. It may even be possible at some point for them to merge into one as we integrate fully our multi-dimensional selves, just as our chakras will ultimately become a single entity. In fact they may even be the equivalent of cosmic chakras!

A nice analogy here is that of a Russian doll. A small wooden figure in the center, symbolizing your physical body in the earthly dimension, is surrounded by increasingly larger-sized hollow replicas, representing your Light bodies in other dimensions.

While the replicas can be independent of one another, it is nevertheless perfectly clear from the similarity of their facial features and attire that they belong together, ideally nestled around the central solid doll to form a distinct unit. In a similar way, your Light bodies can combine in exquisite beauty, resonating harmoniously like a divine musical chord.

The idea behind the next ceremony is to make contact with your Light bodies. The image of fairy lights on a Christmas tree suddenly being lit up when the power is switched on comes to mind here. Alternatively you may prefer to think of it in terms of connecting with the celestial aspects of your being which reside at increasingly higher frequencies along the continuum of Love consciousness.

The wording is quite plain, but it can certainly pack a punch. Here is the heart of it – I leave you to top and tail. You could also acknowledge your Light bodies one by one – ask your higher self for relevant information if need be:

Through Divine Light and Grace, in the Name of Love, through All that I AM, I ask that I be attuned with as many aspects of my being as is suitable for me right now – with each of my Light bodies in every dimension – and that they be brought into melodious balance, perfectly synchronized and connected to one another. (x3)

I AM my multi-dimensional self. I now have complete freedom of access to my divine centres of learning. May the love from these realms spread through my being and emanate from me each day, bringing hope, peace, knowledge, wisdom, compassion and understanding to those who are not yet aware of the existence of other dimensions. (x3)

To recap: your connection with your Light bodies will become firm and secure, allowing a free flow of energy through your multifaceted self. You will have the facility to access talents and intelligence from various perspectives.

Having opened yourself up in this way, and brought even more of your vast potential online, you are well-equipped to bring about change in the world. As already mentioned, this is because the frequencies you emit will travel unimpeded, like an electric current flowing along a wire, to other beings who are also linked to you and your Light bodies via the lattice.

So, for example, if you wish to send love, the most powerful current in the universe, to another realm, perhaps the animal kingdom, not only might you have a Light body which resonates especially well with this domain and knows how best to pass on your communication (it contains the sum of all your expertise in this area), your message will be received loud and clear because you have repaired rusty interdimensional links.

The more spiritual knowledge we have and the higher we vibrate, the greater our number of "live" contacts with the cosmic lattice – and the greater our accountability: we need to use our strength wisely for the good of everyone.

Working with crystals

Let's return to crystals again. Many people are attracted to their healing properties and for some folk these can be utilized in imaginative and ingenious ways.

A few years ago Marcus, a qualified acupuncturist, a very talented astrologer and a deeply spiritual man, rose bravely to the challenge of performing acupuncture on the earth's core at Akutan in the Aleutian Islands, an area where nuclear weapons were tested between 1946 and 1958.

According to Marcus, "The explosions and fall-out caused energetic disturbance to the Earth's energy grids, allowing unbalanced energies, frequencies and entities to enter into our dimensional reality, and influence human consciousness, in a not very positive or healthy way."

Following higher guidance and undeterred by the enormity of what they were undertaking, he and a group of friends embarked on a very special journey. Once they had arrived on the island, settled in and chosen the exact site (pinpointed with a "location crystal"), they next prepared the ground and themselves with a cleansing ceremony during which 97 assorted crystals were lovingly laid out in a series of concentric rings.

The following day they then conducted another improvized ceremony to bring in healing cosmic energy via themselves and the crystals which culminated in a remarkable experience. Marcus describes it in his own words:

...a spiral of deep volcanic red, rose and crimson tones flowed up from within the Earth and for just a second or two, there appeared the most beautiful image of the Divine Mother, in all her youth, beauty, strength, power, subtlety, vulnerability, sorrow, joy and deep ageless wisdom, expressed in that instant of opening and closing her eyes, as the image flowed up to merge with the down-pouring light frequencies from above; this was accompanied by a huge sense of relief and gratitude, mine and hers and the Universe's – there was no separation in that moment…

You don't have to travel thousands of miles or work on a large scale with crystals to enjoy a close, rewarding relationship with them. You can do a great deal with just one or two gems within your home, and in your garden too.

If you are drawn to the mineral kingdom and would like to know how you can best interact with it, you might use the following to further develop communication channels that were established in the Light bodies' attunement:

Through All that I AM I invoke the God/Goddess of crystals and the crystal masters and gatekeepers, and open my heart to you in love and with gratitude. (x3)

Through Divine Law and Grace please show me, with clarity and insight, how I may best learn how crystal, rock, stone and mineral consciousnesses interact with the rest of creation on Mother Earth. May I be allowed access to your kingdom and to share in your celebrations of life in whatever way is appropriate for our highest spiritual benefit and development. (x3)

May our path together be illuminated through laughter, delight, abundance and mutual understanding. Blessings and love to you always. Thank you. (x3)

This invocation/attunement could also be adapted for other realms, including the elemental and angelic, in which case you might weave the following in – although the next paragraphs could also be used as a stand-alone on a separate occasion if you wanted a different slant to your attunement:

> Through Divine Light and Grace, in the Name of God, through All that I AM, I ask that I be fully attuned now to the crystal, elemental, animal, insect, angelic and other higher dimensions of Love and Light, and that through our co-operation humanity becomes more receptive to wisdom gained by other realms in the universe. (x3)
>
> May our friendships be blessed with co-creative projects which bring joy and understanding. May Love shine out from us, promoting expansion of minds and hearts. (x3)
>
> May my words and actions lovingly reflect my deepest appreciation of my non-human friends and our gifts from Spirit. (x3)

You might also try holding a crystal of your choice and asking it directly in your mind or out loud what you can do together. (Always acquire those which attract your attention and "speak" to your heart – this may not necessarily be the biggest or the brightest.) Treat it with affection and courtesy in the same manner as you would a close friend and you may receive some interesting responses.

I do not profess to know very much about crystals, but I have come to admire the gentleness and mastery of these beings who are so keen to contribute to the raising of consciousness.

Several years ago while meandering across the beach at Lyme Regis, renowned worldwide for its abundance of fossils – most notably dinosaur bones – I literally bumped into a largish piece of pale-colored rock. As it had attracted my attention, I scrutinized it more carefully and discovered that at one end it contained a huge amount of a pale lilac crystal which caught the light and glittered like a burst of tiny stars.

It was so gorgeous that I took it home with me where it sat on a shelf near the desk in my office for months on end. I admired it and enjoyed feeling its cold contours under my fingers, but I did not know what else to do with it. Then one day I decided it must have come into my life for a reason, and not just to look pretty for my sake. I picked it up, laid it on my knees, and opened my mind to its frequencies.

A bout of rapid eye movement and whirring sensations inside my body told me information was being imparted. I soon deduced that the rock and crystal presence was requesting that I should invite Archangel Metatron to download it with keys, codes and the such like which it could in turn download to "other beings on, under, in and above Mother Earth, and to Earth herself". I sensed that its more immediate role lay in assisting non-human beings to raise their vibrations, which of course would then indirectly affect humanity too.

Although this was new territory for me, I did not question the rock crystal's desire. I invoked Archangel Metatron and trusted everything would be taken care of. However, the next day I wondered whether my imagination might have got the better of me. Pushing doubts to one side, I called Louise, hoping we could meet and put the rock crystal to the test. Without any hesitation she agreed and so I drove over to her house straight away.

As soon as I placed the portion of rock in her living room, her eyes doubled in size and she did not move a muscle. Her attention was riveted to a blue energy at the pointed end which then traveled along to the crystal section from where small "globules" of a similar blue energy emerged. These rolled along and into the carpet, before vanishing.

For an experiment we chose a few smaller crystals to put on top of the rock crystal – there is a notch which holds them perfectly. First of all, though, we clasped them in our hands to get a sense of their own unique energy. Then we placed them in the notch and continued to watch. As before, the rock end seemed to power up for a few seconds before the crystal section emitted short bursts of energy. Afterwards there was a noticeable difference in the small crystals – somehow they felt clearer.

It so happened that we were giving a talk the following week, and we thought it would be an excellent opportunity to conduct a further experiment by inviting other people to bring their crystals along and put them on or near the Lyme piece for the evening. We waited to explain our reasons to the group until the very end of the session.

Once everyone had reclaimed their crystals, we solicited feedback and were soon gratified to hear exclamations of surprise and comments such as "It feels so much lighter," and "It's bubbling and fizzing with lovely energy," as members of the audience quickly picked up on subtle and not so subtle changes.

The next day the rock crystal was again brought under the spotlight at a workshop, and once more the group could detect a raising of their crystals' vibrations. As I was retelling the anecdote about how and where it was found, a lady named Yvonne gasped in a moment of recognition.

Beaming from ear to ear, she went on to explain how she had recently been guided to work with rock spirits at Lyme Regis through the medium of her painting. In a quiet lull after lunch, she brought out of her bag a picture she had painted, to show me what she meant. The image of a wise, ancient face composed of a blend of fabulous hues of blue stunned me into a humbled silence. We both felt an instant deep connection.

It suddenly seemed quite evident why the chain of events involving Archangel Metatron should have been set in motion by the rock crystal, because it could quite easily have requested a downloading on its own, without my intercession. However, if it had done that, I would not have learned about its broader mission and those of its kind. It was teaching about the desire of beings in all realms and dimensions to interact compassionately with one another on both the small and the grand scale.

Perhaps its most important message is that, if we do not already do so, we should spend a little time trying to think, hear and see beyond the blur that can become daily living. We may be being called upon to act as facilitators – to lend a hand in a most thrilling way we may not have considered before. But we may be being so busy and preoccupied that we are taking for granted or missing the blessings of nature that are revealing themselves right in front of us. Perhaps the crystals you popped in a cupboard for safe keeping all those months ago might have a message for you...

Raising our awareness is also about being receptive and remaining alert and sensitive enough to notice and interpret often subtle signs. There is divine magic everywhere all the time – by being truly ourselves, relaxed and true to our spirit, we can more easily discern it.

Quartz crystals
I shall now concentrate on quartz crystals because their spiritual properties lend themselves well to another interesting form of healing.

Quartz in particular has the capacity to receive, access, store, transmit, amplify and activate all manner of codes, symbols, messages and information from many dimensions. It can process data and pass it on in a form that will be readily assimilated. (It often reminds me of that handy *Star Trek* gizmo, a fictional "universal translator" which enabled most alien species from most galaxies to understand each other's language and to communicate with one another.) In addition, quartz can aid communication between our higher and lower self by temporarily activating our third eye.

I tend to use clear quartz, but you might prefer the colored variations, and I also tend to opt for a reasonably sized piece. Again, though, I have used small crystals to great effect, so there is no hard and fast rule.

With its permission, your crystal can transfer to you information it currently holds. You can also request that it be downloaded by the ascended realms with further appropriate material for you and for anyone else who may come into contact with it. Be specific if there is something you are especially interested in.

Crystals make excellent participants in ceremonies and during invocations because their potent, loving vibrations lend caring support for you. They are also catalysts for change. For instance, renouncing former vows can make you go off-kilter momentarily, but it can be very comforting if you hold a crystal and place it on whichever chakra or part of your body calls for it. I have known people put their crystal to their third eye and heart center and to experience a range of emotions and feelings while making these declarations of intent:

> I AM my multi-dimensional self. Through my I AM Presence I now renounce all vows of poverty, lack and limitation that I have ever expressed in past, present and future lifetimes and realities, including parallel and alternative realities. I invoke the full power of the Violet Flame to transmute their energy, their effects on my being and my poverty consciousness, and to transform them back to divine potential. I ask that my I AM Presence fill the void where the frequencies of poverty existed with the golden Light of God's abundance, prosperity, peace and happiness.

While we're on the subject again, a simpler alternative is:

> I AM my multi-dimensional self. Through All that I AM and with the blessing of this crystal, I now let go of my beliefs in lack, limitation and poverty, and replace them with an understanding of and ability to co-create abundance through God's love.

or even this, which has been known to precipitate a massive Metatron moment:

Dear crystal – please download me with information for abundance!

Round about the time I was researching quartz crystals, I came across a couple of unrelated books whose authors talked about "implants". Even though I should know better, my initial reaction was to scoff and turn quickly to other chapters. As with many topics debated in spiritual circles, however, it is really a question of language and interpretation.

Some people believe implants are devices placed within human bodies by extraterrestrial alien species intent on monitoring our activities in order to learn about life on another planet. I do not have any experience that enables me to comment, so I would prefer to focus instead on two other definitions of implant.

The first encompasses habitual fear-based thought patterns and behaviors that have become so engrained they are like a computer program's default setting which prevents us from moving on.

The second comprises those blocks or controls we either intentionally or unknowingly may have placed on ourselves, perhaps in past lives, to prevent us taking certain courses of action.

These could have stemmed from any type of rash statement we made in reaction to an emotional or distasteful event, such as "I'm never going there again because I had such a horrid time," or "I'm never doing *that* again." (In some respects they are another form of vow, albeit a heat-of-the-moment one.) Or they may be the equivalent of energetic barriers placed by our higher self across our spiritual path until we are mature enough to handle the finer vibrations of a higher evolutionary stage.

In whatever way you explain these blockages and whichever words you use to describe them, you can link with your crystal to remove them. Louise and I conducted a few tests to prove the hypothesis. As she is such an evolved soul and as fit as a fiddle, her experiences were felt on a very refined level. It was a case of undergoing gentle but convincing shifts. My experiences on the other hand were, as usual, more overtly dramatic.

We tried one exercise which addressed the clearing of blocks from our subtle bodies. Louise's clairvoyance came to the fore and she watched spiritual energy in the form of human figures, including that of a Samurai warrior, superimpose themselves over my face.

I had no accompanying sensations, but we guessed these characters were energetic facets from previous lives coming forward for healing – and to confirm that some kind of transformation was taking place.

Although this unexpected phenomenon was most welcome, I nevertheless felt we needed to broaden our request to take account of our physical bodies too, and so we arrived at what I am going to suggest for you.

First of all select your crystal, ask it whether it is happy to work with you and, if so, cleanse it by invoking the violet flame. Then program it by holding it in your right hand (it can be either hand, but some people prefer to use right, then left) and speaking out loud or in your head:

I AM my multi-dimensional self. Through All that I AM, I invoke the crystal masters of Light, cosmic beings of Light, Archangel Metatron etc... and I call upon this dear crystal. (x3)

Under the Law of Grace and in the Name of Love, I command that this crystal be downloaded with codes, keys and other appropriate energy that will remove and transmute into Love and Light fear-based programs, redundant energetic signatures and implants that are no longer serving the highest good of anyone who holds it. (x3)

Wait a few seconds or however long your intuition tells you, transfer your crystal to your left hand. Continue with:

I now ask this crystal to transmit to me appropriate codes, symbols and information for my highest spiritual growth, and also to facilitate the removal from my body, subtle bodies and being all fear-based programs, redundant energetic signatures and implants that are no longer serving my best interests. May they be transmuted through the Violet Flame into Love and Light. I also ask that Love and Light fill the void. (x3)

May such codes, symbols and information as I receive in this ceremony be transformed by the Power of the Violet Flame into Love and Light once they have served their purpose and they are no longer required for my mission. (x3)

I thank my friends for their help and love. May God bless you. (x3)

I have to admit that as I waited in Louise's snug armchair, with a crystal in one hand and in the other a scrap of paper with a hastily scrawled decree, I was extremely dubious about the whole affair. That was until two short, exceedingly forceful and, in the short term, painful, blasts of energy shot through the middle of my body from front to back. What seemed like pockets of air evaporated from my limbs. It was like being hit by a mini bomb blast. The point was definitely made. Whatever it was that had been removed from me, I did not need to know the details. I trusted that all was in perfect divine order.

Since then I have continued to be amazed by what a magnificent array of abilities crystals have, and we are probably only seeing the proverbial tip of the iceberg. (You can re-program your crystals at any time. Always maintain the same high level of spiritual hygiene for them as you do for yourself.) Only recently I bought a group of large quartz crystals which had grown together on a common base. When I tuned into them, I found out that each has a specific effect on the human body: one to balance the right side, one the left, and one to work on the mid-line down the spine. How terrific is that?

I hope if nothing else this chapter provides you with a few ideas to help you spread the joy of crystal healing to many more people and to look afresh at those sometimes neglected beings who may have been quietly sharing your home with you but who may be bursting with enthusiasm to share so much more with you.

Chapter 9

Healing of ancestral energy

Our choice of body, parents, where we were born and many of the people we come into contact with during our life was made very prudently by our soul before we incarnated. It knows which situations will present us with the best conditions for learning, spiritual growth and, for those involved in cancelling out past debts, karmic clearing.

These may come as external challenges, such as being faced with squabbling neighbors or having to sort out an unexpected financial nosedive. Others may be construed as internal codes within our subtle bodies and physical body, perhaps in our DNA, which when activated give rise to ailments.

Both are an integral part of our personal realities, and as such are neither internal nor external, merely tags within our energetic make-up which cause us to search beyond the obvious to restore balance.

In addition, just as we inherit DNA from our parents, so we may also inherit some of their emotions and "negative" karma they were unable to resolve satisfactorily before we were born. It is believed we may even receive energetic remnants from up to nine generations before us. That potentially is a great deal of clutter!

As mentioned in Chapter 3, there may be some individuals who agreed before incarnating that they would transform ancestral karma as part of their service to Mother/Father God. In effect their aim is to sift out the debris from humanity's universal blueprint that is constantly being thrown up from fear-based ways of living.

Regular spiritual practices will enable you to transmute lower vibrational energy of your own. But when it comes to sweeping up after other people, I would remind anyone who thinks this is their lifelong mission to look very carefully at whether it is still an appropriate role for them.

Today enlightened masters agree they must be answerable for their actions. As I've hinted at before, maybe it is also time for us to transform the energetic cycle of suffering into one of mutual love and support by relinquishing self-sacrifice. As every wise parent knows, in the end children have to be allowed to fly the nest and make their own mistakes. You never stop caring for them, but that does not mean you should always rush in whenever they metaphorically trip over.

For compassionate beings this can be a tough direction to take. Nurturing our companions comes so naturally (especially if you have had past lives centered around devotion and abstinence for expected spiritual reward) that denying yourself abundance and freedom may be such an automatic response there is no real desire to alter it. And some people find it easier to love fellow beings than to love themselves.

Always putting others first may, ironically, manifest in your physical body not only as an inferiority complex but as irrational feelings of superiority over others. Or you may be totally unaware of your old programming. You can use Word Power to discover where exactly you stand on the subject by starting with:

"I love others more than myself," or
"I love myself more than others."

Repeat these phrases many times over. You may expose religious vows you took in former lives or alternatively you may find you have further self-worth issues to address.

Unconditional love in the greater scheme of God's creation has an even higher vibration than that of compassion. The ideal way of loving unconditionally is to allow others to achieve their mastery through their own efforts. They are ready, and merely need our encouragement and, perhaps from time to time, our guidance.

This is a straightforward attitude to adopt towards those currently in incarnation. But what about folk who have passed over? Can our unconditional love have an impact on them too? Yes, of course, and we can bring it about quite inventively. For example, you can present your ancestors with the opportunity, should they need or wish it, of taking back and transmuting the energetic residue of their past actions – rather like the multi-dimensional spring cleaning described in Chapter 4. This is not a selfish act on your part. Quite the contrary.

In the following ceremony designed to deal specifically with ancestral energy you can accomplish a huge amount simply by adopting the stance of loving detachment. The phrase "self-empowerment" tends to be overused these days, but that in effect is what we are talking about here.

You make a positive statement to the universe about no longer wishing to carry around the fall-out of your forebears' actions unless it is in your highest spiritual interests – it may, after all, be having an adverse impact on your current health and wellbeing.

Rather than cutting the energy adrift in an irresponsible manner and neglecting the possible needs and welfare of your ancestors, you then ask that it be either "returned to sender(s)", with appropriate healing for the being(s) concerned, or trans-muted by the violet flame and returned to Source. You leave it to the higher realms to determine the best course of action.

Read the ceremony through several times to make sure it represents your truth. You might invite your ancestors to take part with you, and imagine everyone standing in a huge circle, holding hands. Invoke the violet flame and call upon healing angels, ascended masters, etc to assist.

Should you become aware of individuals finding it difficult to adjust to the energetic changes, stand firm in your position of Love and Light and focus on surrounding them with the violet flame. Also request additional help from the celestial planes.

Under the Law of Grace and in the Name of Love, through All that I AM I now release from my physical body and subtle bodies the energy that has been passed down to me from my beloved ancestors, including that which is preventing me from following my divine blueprint for perfect health and wellbeing. (x3)

Through All that I AM, I invoke the Violet Flame and Fire of Light to transmute, transform and return to Source as appropriate this energy – which may be in the form of energetic ties and signatures, past experiences, karma and karmic residues – as well as any other low vibrational codes and patterns which are not my responsibility and/or no longer serve my highest good. (x3)

I also request that any beings who have generated karmic or low vibrational energetic patterns which have been stored in my earthly body and subtle bodies, and who are being adversely affected by the consequence of their actions or to whom it is in their highest interests to take back their own energy, receive guidance on how to bring about healing for themselves. May they be restored to wholeness and surrounded by Love and Light always. (x3)

Under the Law of Grace and in the Name of Love, I request that karmic issues coded within my body and subtle bodies which are my responsibility, or for which I agreed at soul level to deal with on behalf of others, and which I have not yet resolved, be brought forward into my life for me to heal and transmute. May the lessons they reveal lead to peace, joy, harmony and balance. (x3)

May my body, DNA and subtle bodies now resonate with my pristine blue print for perfect health. May all levels of my being vibrate with God's white print for unconditional love. (x3)

May cycles of suffering that exist within humanity's domain be transformed through Love into mutual support and co-operation. (x3)

Thank you dear ancestors for paving the way of Light. Thank you dear Mother/Father God for your multitude of blessings. (x3)

So be it. So it is done. So it is.

It is curious that much interest in family history research has been generated recently: delving into past lineages seems to appeal to people's imaginations the world over. I wonder whether these activities are also transforming ancestral karma in some way. Perhaps through recognizing the existence of our forebears, by sketching in a few of the details of their earthly lives, we are touched by their humanity. And the loving, empathetic responses they often elicit from us reach out to them, bringing recognition and understanding on both sides. That, maybe, is enough to start transmuting lingering regrets, heartache and sadness.

Chapter 10

Flying high

The attunement contained in this chapter is a gift from the higher dimensions and has the potential to initiate wholesale shifts on both the inner and outer planes. As it had such an intriguing genesis, I should like to take a few moments to describe briefly the factors leading up to its creation.

Paul's younger son made the bold decision to leave his job in England temporarily and spend eight months living and working in Peru. He and his girlfriend chose to set up their home in Cusco, the old capital of the Inca Empire in the south-east of the country and only a relatively short hop from Machu Picchu.

They encouraged friends and members of the family to visit them during their stay, and naturally most leapt at the opportunity. Although I would have loved to have gone, my poor health at that time meant it was out of the question. Paul and I discussed pros and cons, and we agreed he should make the trip without me, taking his elder son instead.

I waved him goodbye, and off he went on what was to be an unforgettable holiday. Life at home continued in the usual fashion – except for one evening when I was alone, listening to some music. There on the carpet in front of me appeared three stars in a diagonal line. And by stars I mean the sort that twinkle in the night sky. The curtains were drawn and I had only a table lamp in the corner of the room as a point of illumination, so their brightness was all the more startling.

Then came a rush of spiritual energy and I felt compelled to rummage around for a writing implement and a piece of paper. Words tumbled into my head and onto the pad I was balancing precariously on my knees. After several minutes, the energy departed and I was left staring at my scrawled notes. The gist of the strange message was that I had received a visit – from whom I was not sure.

Almost two years later I was woken shortly before midnight by three bright lights in the bedroom, again in a distinctive slanting line. They each had the intensity of a car's headlights, but as before the curtains were pulled tight shut and this time the house inside and outside was in complete darkness. I drifted off to sleep and my dreams were punctuated by blocks of colors – luminous magenta and emerald green. While the visual aspect was spectacular, even more incredible was that I could actually *feel* these colors profoundly.

Shortly afterwards I had another lucid dream lasting no more than a few seconds in which a picture of a spiral galaxy hove into view. I knew I was meant to take notice of this distinct image, but it baffled me why my attention should have been drawn to what I assumed was the Milky Way.

A propos of nothing a friend forwarded me details of a website she felt would be of interest. I eventually latched onto a page which set my skin pricking with goose bumps and tears flowing down my cheeks. I could not fathom why. It contained no more than a guided meditation from a being calling itself "Mirachi", and various illustrations whose color theme was blue.

Nothing remarkable there, you would think. Nevertheless I was reacting very strongly to something. Frustratingly I could not establish who this Mirachi was, so after a while I left the room, still greatly puzzled.

That evening, lying warmly cocooned in bed, my thoughts returned to the stars which had manifested in the house in such a theatrical way on two separate occasions. I questioned my higher self about what these signified. Within a split second "Andromeda" sounded unequivocally in my head. Apart from having watched a sci-fi series of that name on television, in which Andromeda was a computer, it meant nothing to me. My curiosity was thoroughly piqued.

The morning could not come soon enough. I was up with the lark and, rather than waiting to turn the computer on, I headed straight for a dictionary for clues. I turned to the entry on Andromeda and was astonished to read: "a constellation in the northern hemisphere lying between Cassiopeia and Pegasus, the three brightest stars being of the second magnitude. It contains the Andromeda Galaxy, a spiral galaxy 2.2 million light years away..."

After gathering myself together, I then had the patience to switch on the computer and search for more information as well as photographs taken with the aid of astronomical telescopes. The very first space shot of the Andromeda Galaxy I hit upon showed three radiant stars, in a line just as I had been shown.

Not only that, I discovered with shock that the second of these stars is called Mirach. I'm sure the neighbors next door must have heard my jaw bouncing up and down off the floor as I furiously pieced together the evidence I had been provided with so meticulously.

During the following weeks there were further pointers and confirmations which led me to throw a few tons of limiting beliefs out of the window and to open my heart to a close connection with galactic higher dimensions that was undoubtedly being established. I had never had a problem with the concept of alien beings living on other planets, perhaps in different realities which is why we may not yet see them, but I had preferred the extraterrestrials in my life to be confined to escapist entertainment. Now, through new experiences filled with deep, sometimes heart-rending, emotion and surfacing memories, I was being asked to consider as my truth the fact that part of me knew about Andromeda – and knew it very well.

After I had recovered some equanimity, a lovely spiritual energy started to show itself regularly. On occasion it seemed that everywhere I looked, there it was – a light, delicate blue color. I was also aware of being fed information, and gradually the idea formulated for an attunement, which I naturally referred to as an "Andromedan attunement".

At first I was hesitant to commit to such an undertaking, because it was so far out of my comfort zone. However, my resistance was rapidly being broken down: the blue energy was like a constant dig in the ribs, and I was having difficulty sleeping because of sheer excitement which kept welling up inside me but which felt as though it was coming from a much higher vibrational part of me. This sounds ridiculous now, but at one point I even asked for the joy to be toned down, as my body was having trouble coping with the elevated frequencies.

One day I received a very definite phrase – "open the gates of consciousness" – to incorporate into the wording and so, having decided to bite the bullet, I sat down and wrote out my ceremony. Although I was tired, I went straight ahead with it there and then, trusting in the divine wisdom that had been guiding me so overtly.

Nothing very unexpected happened during the subsequent meditation, but the same could not be said of the night's experiences which punctuated my sleep. The culmination was a vision of an indeterminate space, perhaps a vast hall, imbued with ethereal blue light, whose brilliance and quality of hue were so transcendently beautiful that it seemed as though God's very Light essence was present. I felt I was glimpsing a higher dimension comprised solely of this sublime, pure, crystalline luminosity.

Then, to my even greater astonishment at something so incomparably exquisite being surpassed, the luminescence and color were dramatically increased several fold. I gasped out loud as I lay there in bed, completely and utterly stunned by the spectacle. Nothing could have prepared me for what I was blessed that evening to witness...

It might sound rather corny to say, but I have never been the same since. Any doubts I had had about the effectiveness of a simple home-made attunement to expand heart and mind had been removed in the most life-transforming of ways.

"Intergalactic" healing attunement

Having said all of this, the nature of the origins of this attunement is in a sense unimportant. Whoever prompted it and from whichever dimension does not really matter either (Andromedan energy is said by some to exist on the sixth dimension, while others suggest the tenth).

The most important point to convey is that its content and potential to impact on your spiritual growth are not dependent on your belief or otherwise in beings from other star systems and realms. See the attunement as a vehicle for sending a message from you to your divine multifaceted self that you are ready to access deeper levels of your consciousness on a more permanent basis.

Check with your heart center that it is right for you and that you are sufficiently prepared for it. As always, the wording printed here is child-like in its simplicity, but potent nevertheless. Please feel free to alter it should you wish to. The key phrases are in italics and can be extracted and used on their own. The request to connect with ET masters is an optional extra for those who are drawn to such activity (see the note at the end of the chapter).

Thanks be to Mother/Father God for All that Is now and always. (x3)

I AM a multi-dimensional being. Through my I AM Presence I invoke the Violet Flame and Violet Fire of Light to transmute energy in and around my being in every dimension, time frame and reality, and to transform it into Light. I AM the Violet Flame. (x3)

Through All that I AM, under the Law of Grace and in the Name of Love, I call upon:

Archangel Metatron, Sanat Kumara, Venus Kumara, the Ascended Masters of Love and Light, the Galactic Masters of Love and Light, interplanetary cosmic beings of Love and Light, Lord Vishnu ("Protector of the Cosmos"), Lord Ashtar and Lords of the Galactic Command (Masters supporting Earth's ascension), cosmic faeries, interdimensional Light Facilitators of codes, symbols and keys, angels and archangels of Love, Light and Healing, my healing guides and mentors, my Andromedan, Pleiadian, Arcturian and Sirian friends, the Galactic High Council, the Andromedan Council, my monad, my soul and any other being of Love and Light who wishes to help this process today. I send you love and gratitude, and ask God to bless you. (x3)

Through All that I AM, under the Law of Grace and in the Name of God, I ask that:

– *I be cleansed and purified gently and easily in preparation for this attunement*

– *the interdimensional and intergalactic gates of consciousness within my being be opened* and that

– if appropriate I be attuned to communicate and work with intergalactic ET masters of Love and Light. (x3)

I thank all beings and energies of Love and Light for their support, empowerment, love and facilitating. (x3)

Thank you God for these marvelous blessings. May all who help me be blessed a thousand fold too. (x3)

Clare, who has very kindly provided feedback for this book, made these observations about happenings in her life shortly after taking the attunement:

I have... had some "insights" whilst doing something relaxing or when my husband Andrew is driving. Some of them seem rather obvious, but the best sense I can make of these is that I am being reminded of things I had forgotten.

For example, I was picking some tomatoes in the greenhouse one day and it struck me that it seemed miraculous that just one tiny seed could turn into a plant bearing many, many tomatoes for our sustenance. If you didn't know what a seed was, you would think it was impossible, and similarly, a tiny fertilized cow egg turns into a hefty beast... I suppose I was being shown some of the miraculous things in my everyday world that perhaps I'd been ignoring for a while.

The next one came in the bathroom, of all places. It occurred to me that we only have the sense organs that we need for the environment we developed in, so we can't really expect to be able to perceive everything in the universe. This is obvious and isn't original, but then I "realized" that to be able to perceive everything in existence, every square inch of our bodies would need to be covered in sense organs, which would be uncomfortable to say the least. The message I got from this is – don't feel frustrated about not being able to see everything that is out there.

The most astonishing insight came whilst I was being driven past a forest, but most of it came through in a non-verbal form. It was a kind of "understanding" about how trees communicate with each other over centuries, using things that we might not recognize as being part of a nervous system. I imagined them respiring, excreting, etc, and thought about some of the chemical exchanges that go on, but from here it all gets rather fuzzy and non-verbal and I'm left not knowing whether or not the chemical exchanges between them are forms of communication, or if communication takes place in some other way. I just seem to "know" that they do communicate, and that a question or a statement from one tree might take decades or centuries to be answered. I seemed to "know" that humans are unusual in wanting/having "fast" conversations.

Serendipity

I always feel doubly blessed when I stumble across supporting evidence after an "event" which validates it and helps to explain it further. In this case about a month after taking the attunement I was drawn to buy a book called *Voices from our Galaxy* by gifted psychic medium Elaine Thompson.

It is a fascinating account of her experiences of meeting with and receiving information from a number of beings from different sections of the universe. One of these is an Andromedan who talks about how it has always been hard for humans to function multi-dimensionally when we are not asleep and dreaming.

I would like to quote one paragraph in particular from Elaine's book which leapt off the page at me. It brought a smile to my face. The words, echoing "gates of consciousness" in the attunement, were spoken by the Andromedan she encountered:

The difficulty comes with crossing the barrier of consciousness. When you leave the dream state and come into your waking conscious state, a mental "safety gate" comes into action, and for the time being, rightly so. We understand that dealing with two realities [*full consciousness, ie dream state, and partial consciousness, ie waking state*] simultaneously is a very difficult thing for humans to maintain. It could feel like a psychosis or madness; as if you were feeling like two different people at the same time. One part of you, knowing how to be free and liberated, and the other part having to eat, work, clean, and do all the physical things that you do every day, and interact with the rest of the world.

It should now be a little clearer why there was such a thrill surrounding the "Andromedan attunement" – not because of the beings themselves, as they would I am sure see themselves as older brothers and sisters who happened to be on the spot to offer advice, but because humanity has made such quantum leaps forward in their evolution that we are now ready to search yet further within ourselves for truths previously far beyond our comprehension.

We are ready for those gates of consciousness to be flung open and taken off their rusty hinges so that we can gain access to complete freedom of spirit *at all times* and not just in the dream state. That is certainly worth celebrating in style.

Note

Many people feel a definite pull towards certain stars and star systems, and may even yearn to go back "home". If you are one of these people and would like to explore such ideas further, Paul McCarthy is currently working with "starseeds", helping them develop their healing, teaching and channeling abilities, and also offering attunements (see Books and websites for his contact details). His definition of starseeds is: "beings that have experienced life elsewhere in the Universe on other planets and in non-physical dimensions. They have come to earth to help and serve others as well as the planet herself."

Chapter 11

Following your dream

Sometimes, even for the experienced spiritual traveler, there may be occasions when your heart's desire seems just that bit too big an apple to pluck from the tree of plenty. In such circumstances it is perfectly natural to think: "That really is impossible," or "This is such a huge ask... I'm sure I'm not meant to have it now."

But hang in there. Check into your heart center to find out where this yearning is coming from. Is it a trick of your lower mind that is plumping up a few of your peacock feathers? If so, it is not worth devoting any more time to it.

Or do you feel at a deep level that your soul has planted a seed within you? If this scenario rings true, then you are being given a golden opportunity in two respects. Firstly, it is a tasty carrot to dangle in front of you to keep you focused and, secondly, it is an excellent opportunity to learn whatever is needed to get you to the point at which you can grab that carrot and devour it with relish. (That's if you still wish to by that stage. A high vibrational target will often draw out of you so much low vibrational material that this is what the process is really all about: you might never actually reach your goal, but you will have great fun along the way and your spiritual learning will progress in leaps and bounds. Not only that, you won't actually mind not getting your carrot!)

As an example, you might have the impulse to uproot yourself and live abroad but do not yet have the confidence, finances or family support to move. Rather than taking the easy option and rejecting the idea as pie in the sky, you could honor your dream and make it happen by creating your own ceremonies.

You might have to step out of your comfy slippers – grow in some new directions, repair the odd relationship, let go of old, stifling beliefs or brush up on a few skills – but it will be nothing you cannot handle. And if the road gets a little bumpy, all you have to do is check in again to your heart center. The odd waver is to be expected but if, under the surface worry and tension, that belief is still there, as solid as ever, keep the momentum going. Your higher self will no doubt continue to prod you in the right direction anyway.

A soul nudge you might contemplate to see if it resonates with you is what may be described as "instantaneous healing", the sort of marvelous restitution to wholeness Jesus is said to have effected, presumably partly through activating a person's blueprint for perfect health – or rather what might be called their "whiteprint", ie their true divine pattern, as a blueprint for our physical bodies may contain DNA irregularities.

In today's climate this sort of healing might be viewed as the ability to channel each strand or ray of God's healing energy available in the physical dimension. In effect that means accessing yet more of our godself, which comprises every facet of divine essence.

While there are undoubtedly fantastic healers with superb healing methods spread around the globe and spontaneous healing does happen, it is still my hope that many more people will be proactive in bringing about healing of themselves in a manner which is consistent with their evolved state of consciousness.

It is too often the case that a person's mind is so keen to govern everything it fears that it does not allow the body to convey its messages, which then prevents the body from doing what it knows best – restoring itself quickly to peak condition, and drawing if need be on God's healing love. After all, each body *is* God, perfectly capable of creating its own miracles.

The mind can also have a vice-like grip because it does not trust the body or the emotions, perhaps as a result of apparently being let down in the past. A mental pattern can become established, the effect of which is to cause the body, whether it likes it or not, to endure imposed forces which may not be in its best interests. It is then even more difficult for an individual to recover long-term equilibrium.

This is why clearing the physical and subtle bodies of energetic blockages, and bringing everything into balance, is so important. As I have tried to demonstrate throughout the book, consciousness exists within every cell and atom and at every level of our being. If our higher and lower minds, spirit and matter, are in agreement, and there are no clogs elsewhere, then energy can flow smoothly and freely for optimum health and vitality.

To give a musical analogy. The higher divine mind is like a composer, brimming with potential and creativity. The lower mind is the equivalent of the conductor who interprets the composer's instructions, while members of the orchestra – the body, comprising its organs and systems, emotions and feelings – create with passion the intricacies of the musical vision.

At times the orchestral players participate together, while at others the woodwind section, the strings or the percussion may come to the fore because that is what is required of them in the composition. For solo pieces the conductor may even step aside for a short while to allow the performer free rein to express themselves fully.

Every musician, from the composer to the tambourine player, is a specialist of sorts, as well as a member of a well-oiled team. In a similar way the professionals within our being must be allowed to pull together when necessary but also to get on with what they each do best when particular circumstances arise.

I am probably being heavily influenced by cognizance of other dimensions in which reality is manifested in the blink of an eye and I realize that there are often complex issues surrounding personal healing. If it is to happen, it can do so slowly so that a person is reminded of how to love and live in their body. Enormous wisdom and strength come through following this sort of path.

While shortcuts are not always the best solution in terms of spiritual growth, a world in which human beings can thrive without quite so many pills, potions and surgical knives is nevertheless a very attractive one and therefore I would like to encourage as many people as possible to review how much they are prepared to develop their gifts for their own personal healing in order to achieve this. To that end I hope some of the material in this book will provide you with helpful suggestions.

Should you like the idea of taking your healing abilities onto a further plane still – to access larger sections of the cosmic lattice permanently rather than briefly during a healing session – you might like to play around with the following decrees: they may uncover a few blockages or at least bring a degree of clarity to your thinking on the subject. By "healing abilities" I mean your way of tapping into and becoming the power of Love. This may or may not involve conventional spiritual healing.

Replace any phrases which do not resonate with you with your own:

I AM that I AM. Through Divine Grace and Light, it is my intention to create perfect health for myself always, and to be able at all times to bring my physical body and energetic bodies into balance and alignment.

It is my intention to create the means through which I can channel each frequency of divine healing energy.

As a spiritual being of infinite love and compassion, I am worthy of healing myself in an instant.

I joyfully let go of old ways of healing and open to new ones.

I am worthy of perfect health now and always.

Once you have tried these, you might then proceed with an attunement such as this:

> Through Divine Grace and in the name of Love, I ask for help in unlocking the infinite potential within my body to heal itself (spontaneously). May my heart and mind be opened to the abundance of cosmic healing energy which radiates from my soul through its divine connection with Mother/Father God. May I now access this bountiful cosmic healing energy freely and easily to support and nourish my being wherever and whenever it is needed. (x3)
>
> May I use my gift of healing for the highest good of every being – that all, under the Law of Grace and through God's abundance, shall benefit according to their needs. (x3)

I wish you joy and much fun in your endeavours. God bless.

Books and websites

These books have more information on some of the material I have outlined in *Open to Love*:

Are you a Master of Light? How to work with new energies from higher dimensions, Louise Hopkinson and Jane White (Bossiney Books, 2004) (www.bossineybooks.com)

Elegant Empowerment: Evolution of Consciousness, Peggy Pheonix Dubro and David P Lapierre (Platinum Publishing, 2002)

The Light Shall Set You Free, Dr Norma Milanovich and Dr Shirley McCune (Athena Publishing, 1996)

ME, Chronic Fatigue Syndrome & Fibromyalgia: The Reverse Therapy® Approach, John Eaton (Authors OnLine Ltd, 2006)

Voices from our Galaxy, Elaine J Thompson (Bright Star Press, 2005) (www.elaine-thompson.com)

Website addresses I came across while writing this book:

www.apsismusic.com ("music for the human spirit" by Anael and Bradfield)

www.crystalinks.com (a comprehensive "metaphysical and science" website)

www.EMFWorldwide.com (information about the work of Peggy Phoenix Dubro, originator of the EMF Balancing Technique® and discoverer of the Universal Calibration Lattice® (Copyright © The Energy Extension Inc. EMF Balancing Technique® All Rights Reserved))

www.healpastlives.com (for information about vows)

www.heavenandearth.org.uk (website of Marcus Mason, astrologer and astro cartographer)

www.reverse-therapy.com (for information about Dr John Eaton's work) www.siriusascension.com (Paul McCarthy is doing excellent work with and for star seeds)

www.vitalaffirmations.com and www.inner-truth.net (helpful information about the causes of illness and the link between mind, body and emotions)

http://web.me.com/theart2heal (website of Graham George, digital artist (see his image on the front cover of this book) and author)

If you have enjoyed *Open to Love*, you might like to visit my website: www.opentolove.info

B O O K S

O is a symbol of the world, of oneness and unity. In different cultures it also means the "eye," symbolizing knowledge and insight. We aim to publish books that are accessible, constructive and that challenge accepted opinion, both that of academia and the "moral majority."

Our books are available in all good English language bookstores worldwide. If you don't see the book on the shelves ask the bookstore to order it for you, quoting the ISBN number and title. Alternatively you can order online (all major online retail sites carry our titles) or contact the distributor in the relevant country, listed on the copyright page.

See our website **www.o-books.net** for a full list of over 500 titles, growing by 100 a year.

And tune in to myspiritradio.com for our book review radio show, hosted by June-Elleni Laine, where you can listen to the authors discussing their books.

MySpiritRadio